Praise for *How I Made It*

Ever wonder whether there is room for "heart" in big business? Meet Tim Moore, an entrepreneurial visionary who made it on his own terms, while helping so many others along the way. Tim is proof positive that a combination of big dreams, hard work, patience, integrity, and generosity of spirit is the ultimate recipe for success. His business savvy has been a great inspiration to me, and his friendship is one I truly treasure.

JEANNE BEKER
Journalist, author, media personality

"As entrepreneurs, we are walking and talking human-interest stories." This quote struck me—it is so true, and it's the Tim Moore I know and the business titan you will "meet" in this book. These stories from his life portray an entrepreneur who is gracious, driven, faith-based, courageous, and ambitious. They are woven in such a way that the book becomes an effective roadmap—a candid guide for aspiring change-makers that offers insightful, raw, honest advice. From my personal and professional experiences with Tim, this poignant reflection is as honest as it is helpful.

KIM MASON
Executive Vice-president, Royal Bank of Canada

Tim Moore is unsinkable. He's a whirling dervish who can't stop moving or talking about it. And lucky we are! Lots of practical advice here on how to build a successful and happy life.

HON. DAVID PETERSON
Former Premier of Ontario; Chancellor Emeritus, University of Toronto

Part memoir, part master class, this uplifting and inspiring page-turner, written with candour and humour, is Tim Moore's story of grit, risk, and resilience, and is proof that hard work, lessons learned, and optimism build success—one bold step at a time!

HON. MYRA FREEMAN, CM, ONS, MSM, CD
Former NS Lieutenant-Governor

In sharing his story, Tim teaches us the life of an entrepreneur is anything but boring. His personal accounts of success, failure, and everything in between shine a light on what it takes to make it big in business. From comical real-life adventures to honest lessons learned, *How I Made It* packs a punch of entrepreneurial spirit and money-making know-how.

STARR CUNNINGHAM ICD.D
President & CEO, Mental Health Foundation of Nova Scotia

How I Made It is an inspiring and insightful book for anyone considering a career as an entrepreneur. Tim Moore's success in business offers lessons about following one's principles, the importance of good decision-making, and the human considerations along the path to success. An enjoyable read.

HON. RUSSELL MACLELLAN
Premier of Nova Scotia 1997–99

Join Tim Moore as he reveals how he built a Canadian success story! Determination, staying power, and the ability to pivot and overcome adversity while maintaining his personal integrity are the hallmarks of his amazing career. *How I Made It* is well worth the read.

HON. LARRY W. SMITH
Senator—Québec

How I Made It is a business memoir full of business and life lessons. Tim Moore, at this stage, has done it all and he has no reason to hold back. He tells it all—and if you're wise, you'll listen.

DANNY MURPHY
President, D. P. Murphy Group of Companies

How I Made It is a powerful and engaging reflection on Tim Moore's entrepreneurial journey, which has been marked by determination, authenticity, and unwavering appreciation for people's character—a trait deeply rooted in family values. Despite the eclectic nature of his business ventures, Moore's story is grounded in principles that transcend personal and financial success. His commitment to hard work and resilience while maintaining a sense of fun make this book not only an inspiring read but also a meaningful guide for aspiring entrepreneurs—proof that success built on integrity, perseverance, and joy is both lasting and deeply fulfilling.

DR. MICHAEL KHAN
President and Vice-chancellor, Saint Mary's University, Halifax, NS

Tim describes what it takes to be successful in business. To become number one in the world in my sport I needed exactly the same things—hard work, grit, persistence, risk, and belief. Tim's journey is the perfect guide to becoming successful in whatever you choose to do.

DIANE JONES KONIHOWSKI CM, LLD (HON)
Former pentathlete

A great book, not just for budding entrepreneurs, but for anyone involved in leadership—in business, in community, and in church. As a parish priest juggling different parishes for more than thirty-three years,

How I Made It resonates with what I have learned, and also with what has challenged me. As Tim says: "A company must be run collaboratively, with a great deal of decision-making power given to the franchise owners—the people who know their individual markets best."

FR. JOHN MACPHERSON
Parish priest

Tim has given us a path to becoming extraordinary. This is not the "Woe is Me" club: This is the "Whoa! It's Me" club! Positive attitude is the hydrogen of success. *How I Made It* proves there is only one person at the controls of your vehicle to success: You! His message—drive with urgency, not recklessly, and respect those who helped you by helping others—will resonate with entrepreneurs. Be the person you want to be in business with.

DR. TOM JACKSON, CC, LLD
Actor, musician, activist
(*Sullivan's Crossing*; *The Huron Carole*)

How I Made It chronicles Tim Moore's very personal life journey of entrepreneurship. The reader lives through the excitement, hard work, and sacrifices of someone who, guided by strong spiritual and family values, sees business opportunities across a spectrum of the economy where others do not. Not all work out, but Moore moves on and learns from the experience. The importance of seeking advice and mentorship are recurring themes, as is the need for leaders to devote their time to nurturing the leaders of tomorrow and their resources to the communities in which they live.

DR. COLIN DODDS
Professor of Finance, Sobey School of Business
Saint Mary's University, Halifax

HOW I MADE IT

Secrets of a Self-Made Multi-Millionaire

HOW I MADE IT

Secrets of a Self-Made Multi-Millionaire

TIM MOORE

Nimbus Publishing Limited
3660 Strawberry Hill Street, Halifax, NS, B3K 5A9
(902) 455-4286 nimbus.ca

Nimbus Publishing is based in Kjipuktuk, Mi'kma'ki, the traditional territory of the Mi'kmaq People. No part of this book may be used in the training of generative artificial intelligence technologies or systems.

Printed and bound in Canada

NB1784

Editor: Paula Sarson
Editor for the press: Angela Mombourquette
Cover design: Heather Bryan
Cover image: Sándor Fizli
Interior design: Bee Stanton
All images courtesy Tim Moore unless otherwise indicated.

"The Station" by Robert Hastings has been reprinted with the generous permission of Southern Illinois University Press.

Library and Archives Canada Cataloguing in Publication

Title: How I made it : secrets of a self-made multi-millionaire / Tim Moore.
Names: Moore, Tim, 1944- author
Identifiers: Canadiana (print) 20250319012 | Canadiana (ebook) 20250319020 | ISBN 9781774715376 (softcover) | ISBN 9781774715383 (EPUB)
Subjects: LCSH: Moore, Tim, 1944- | LCSH: Success in business. | LCSH: Entrepreneurship. | LCSH: Businesspeople—Canada—Biography.
Classification: LCC HF5386 .M66 2026 | DDC 650.1—dc23

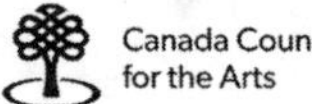

Nimbus Publishing acknowledges the financial support for its publishing activities from the Government of Canada, the Canada Council for the Arts, and from the Province of Nova Scotia. We are pleased to work in partnership with the Province of Nova Scotia to develop and promote our creative industries for the benefit of all Nova Scotians.

For Bernardine, my best friend and soulmate,
to whom I owe much of my success.

Contents

Foreword

TIM MOORE HAS GUTS. THAT'S WHAT MADE HIM SUCCESSFUL. Simple as that. He started with nothing—nothing except his drive to make money and be successful. But to sustain that drive and build on it with others, he needed something else: leadership skills. Tim has an innate gift as a leader, a quality in short supply these days.

Many of today's largest businesses had humble beginnings. That's not new. But many entrepreneurs and management executives tend to expound about how great it is to start a business and how well they did. They're on a victory lap, burnishing their reputations.

Tim, on the other hand, is down-to-earth, brutally honest about how hard it is to run a business and scale up. He has experienced setbacks. He has made both sacrifices and mistakes. He has navigated crises. He has mentored good employees—and managed bad ones.

I have known Tim for over forty years. He has integrity and a strong moral compass. I have marvelled at his remarkable work ethic, his quick decisiveness, his considered approach to risk, and his charming manner that together have made people want to work with him and turned clients into loyal friends of his brand of service.

Of particular note is that Tim founded more than one company. He's not a one-trick pony. He is a serial entrepreneur who developed a knack for identifying gaps in the marketplace that his ideas could fill. A lot of that knack was based on "gut feel." He researched companies and business sectors, but his greatest skills were intuition and observation.

He began as a midnight driver with a makeshift tarp-covered moving truck. Then he founded AMJ Campbell and within ten years built it into Canada's largest national moving company. He went on to found Premiere Executive Suites, Premiere Van Lines, and other Premiere brand companies, including Premiere Mortgage Centre and Premiere Self Storage. He launched into the alternative lending business with Atlantic Signature Mortgage & Loan and, just recently, Maritime Edge Mortgage. (An entrepreneur never retires, apparently.) Along the way, he got into the luxury resort sector by buying and transforming the Oceanstone Resort on Nova Scotia's captivating Atlantic coast.

In this book, Tim unpacks his secrets with humour, honesty, and astute insights, making it a valuable reference for both fledgling and experienced entrepreneurs in dealing with employees, family members in the business, partners, banks, the government, and competitors.

More than anything, he proves that good guys can finish first. At a time when toxic leadership in the world is a source of great anxiety, Tim reminds us that hard work, motivation of others, and the creation of a corporate culture that feels like a close family unit are key components of success. He was a tough leader, don't get me wrong. He had to be. But he has been a leader with heart, unique in his drive to help enrich his employees and have fun while doing it. Dozens of his partners became millionaires under his guidance. Indeed, that may be his greatest legacy.

Tim was not in business solely for himself. He was in business to create something valuable and cherished not only for investors but also for those who worked alongside him.

Mark Borkowski

President, Mercantile Mergers & Acquisitions Corporation

Foreword

FROM A CEDAR-SHINGLED PERCH ABOVE MAHONE BAY, with ferries chugging to Tancook and squalls visible on the horizon, Tim Moore invites us into a vantage point that is both literal and figurative. The view from his crescent-shaped home in Chester, Nova Scotia, is wide—like the sweep of a life spent building, rebuilding, and building again. That image is the right way to enter this book because perspective is Tim's superpower: the ability to see storms forming early, to read the water, and to set a course with grit and composure.

Tim doesn't arrive on these pages as the polished tycoon you might expect. He starts with nothing—and then starts again. He writes candidly about failing grades, leaving the seminary after three years, and a first marriage that didn't last. He tells the stories most business books skip: the nosebleed that wouldn't stop after working two twenty-hour shifts, the chain-gang track work in Northern Ontario, the times he was broke and needed the next job to appear. And then there's the tradesman who assumed Tim was the gardener and asked him to move the Jeep blocking the drive. (Tim moved it.) That moment of mistaken identity isn't a punchline; it's the book in miniature. Humility is not an affect here—it's operating principle and edge.

The achievements are real and considerable: transforming a one-truck operation at age twenty-one into AMJ Campbell Van Lines, Canada's largest mover with a thousand trucks on the road and $125 million in annual revenue at its peak; creating Premiere Executive Suites, the country's largest extended-stay accommodations business with more than twelve hundred furnished units and twenty offices; co-founding Premiere Van Lines; launching Premiere Mortgage Centre, later Atlantic Signature Mortgage & Loan; building and selling Premiere Self Storage for $13.5 million; turning Oceanstone from a money-losing resort into a beloved Nova Scotia destination. But Tim refuses to tell a triumphalist tale. Alongside the scale-ups and rankings are the misfires and stumbles: a nursing-home investment that didn't work, an advance-payments venture that turned out to be a Ponzi scheme, debt, reversals, and the hard exits that test character.

What, then, holds the story together? For me, three things.

First, work ethic with direction. Tim quotes Helen Keller—character forged in trial and suffering—and then shows the receipts: paper routes, doughnut wagons, CN boxcars, the discipline of sport, and later the discipline of leadership. Work alone can exhaust; work aimed at a standard becomes culture. You feel that in how he hires, trains, and insists on "finishing early" by doing the hard thing first.

Second, financial realism. Growing up amid money stress and two family bankruptcies left a scar that became a strength. Tim obsesses—in the best sense—about cash, debt, dilution, and risk. In an era when slogans can replace spreadsheets, his pages are refreshingly frank about the arithmetic of survival.

Third, the authority of humility. The Chester anecdote, the "who the hell is Tim Moore?" furniture-truck story his wife loves to tell, the reminder that you're never as important as you think—these aren't cute asides. They explain why people follow Tim. Humility keeps leaders curious. It keeps them listening to mentors, learning from crews on the floor, and calibrating when the wind shifts.

The book is also—quietly but importantly—about decoding your past. Tim asks colleagues about their upbringing because he's done that work himself. He understands how childhood—strict parents, scarce praise, a home that looked prosperous while creditors called—can wire our fears and ambitions. That self-awareness runs through his advice: learn where your reflexes come from, then decide which to keep.

Entrepreneurs will find a practical playbook here: act early in a storm, keep powder dry, choose the right partners, protect culture, face problems directly, and never outsource your judgment. But non-entrepreneurs will find something too. Tim writes for anyone who wants more agency in uncertain times: keep your composure, narrow your focus, work the problem, and—crucially—define the level of success you actually want. Not everyone needs to be "top dog." Clarity beats status.

Tim is candid about the world our next generation faces—AI reshaping work, climate risk, geopolitical jolts, trade frictions—but he refuses despair. Change, he argues, is the entrepreneur's invitation. Needs shift; opportunities appear. Read, listen, observe; then ship something of value. That optimism isn't naïveté. It's earned by weathering enough cycles to know that markets and lives both move in seasons.

Most business autobiographies are either sanitized or sermonizing. This one is neither. It is human—funny in places, bracing in others, full of specific numbers and specific names, with detours into the seminary, sport, family, and faith that add depth rather than decoration. You will come away with tactics, yes, but also with a feel for what stamina actually looks like in a life: beginning again, and again, without bitterness.

If you're starting out, this book will shorten your learning curve. If you're mid-career, it will help you re-centre on the few levers that matter. If you're on your third act, it will remind you that reinvention is not a slogan but a practice.

From that hill above Mahone Bay, you can see weather coming long before it arrives at the dock. Read this book the same way: as an early warning system, a set of charts, and with confidence that—even when the sky darkens—there's always a way to tack toward home.

Brian Crombie
Corporate finance strategist; real estate development executive; media host: *The Brian Crombie Hour*

Nothing in the world can take the place of persistence. Talent will not; nothing is more common than unsuccessful men with talent. Genius will not; unrewarded genius is almost a proverb. Education will not; the world is full of educated derelicts. Persistence and determination are omnipotent. The slogan "press on!" has solved and always will solve the problems of the human race.

CALVIN COOLIDGE
President of the United States, 1923–29

Introduction

I WRITE FROM MY HOME IN CHESTER, NOVA SCOTIA, WHERE the view is wide. Situated on a steep hill at the tip of a peninsula and shaped in a crescent, the cedar-shingled house has multiple terraces that overlook Mahone Bay on the province's South Shore. The bay is a picturesque and storied expanse of water with hundreds of islands, many uninhabited, some with reputed pirate treasure. My wife, Bernardine, and I bought the property in 1988, where we would design and build our forever home. From this vantage point, we can watch the sun rise and set. Boats pass by. A ferry to Tancook Island chugs along its route several times a day. Flocks of migrating birds swoop through. We witness the changing moods of the sea. On the far horizons, we can even see squalls forming and rainstorms or fair skies that will soon come our way. We have a rare perspective, in other words. A valuable perspective.

That's how I also feel about my fifty-year career as an entrepreneur. I started with nothing.

The other day, a tradesman drove through the gates of our property and travelled partway down our sloping drive. He had come to fix a pipe. My Jeep was blocking him from proceeding closer to the house. He got out of his van, hands on hips, and spied me in the garden, where I was looking for a tool in a shed. Assuming that I was an employee, he hollered over to ask if I could move my Jeep.

"Sure, no problem," I replied, then quickly went to fetch my keys.

Once the driveway was cleared, he moved his van forward, parked, and got out. "You live here?" he asked incredulously, having watched me go in through the front door of the house to get my car keys. "You're the owner?" he continued, slightly embarrassed that he mistook me for a gardener. (I was dressed casually!)

"Yes," I replied.

"How'd you afford this place—rob a bank?" he blurted.

I burst into laughter. *Maritimers are refreshingly direct!* I thought.

"No, no," I replied with a chuckle. "I started a couple of businesses."

I'll be honest when I tell you that there are still some days when I'm just as surprised as that tradesman about what I've been able to achieve. I had no formal business education. I had an extremely unpromising start. I failed grade 3. I dropped math in grade 10. I failed grade 12, forced to repeat it. Then I failed grade 13 with a 35 percent average. Embarrassing to admit.

My drive? The need to make money. Fast. I was hungry for success, desperate in some ways, and determined. I was never afraid of hard work. And I had to survive.

I want to share what I have learned over the last half a century, not just to encourage young people who are starting out and thinking about founding a business but also because I hope there's some reassurance in the notion of the will and energy to survive. It's what Canada now faces with the threat of the Trump administration. As I listen to business people and politicians express their worries over how the country will manage tariffs and other obstructionist policies from our southern neighbour, I reflect on how many principles of business—and my own experience—are instructive and inspiring:

- Work hard.
- Have grit.
- Be persistent.
- Take calculated risks.
- Hold belief.
- Find solutions in a crisis.
- Listen to mentors who are smarter and more experienced than you.
- Work together for a common purpose.
- Define your leadership.

Those are some of the keys to success. Sound easy? Maybe when you write them in a tidy list as I just have. In practice, it is a challenging, exhausting, exhilarating—and sometimes messy—adventure, which I will tell you about in this book.

To be sure, the younger generation faces challenges that I never did. These include, for instance, the advent of artificial intelligence and how it will upend the labour market, eliminating some jobs. Climate change. Economic uncertainty. A global political reordering that creates anxiety. But here's the truth. Everything is always changing. That is life. That is business. Identifying opportunities is always an entrepreneur's focus. And when change is afoot, I would argue that even more opportunities arise. People's needs change. To stay attuned to these evolving opportunities is about paying close attention to what people need now. Read. Listen. Observe. What do they want? How can you bring a product or a service that meets the demands of this moment in our culture?

The great advantage of being an entrepreneur is that you have some control of your future. In a time of economic uncertainty, this is extremely valuable. No one can fire you or make you redundant. You own the business you create. You make sacrifices for it. You work hard for it.

When people talk to me about the difficulties and different challenges facing the next generation, I understand and empathize. And then I say this: I'm an eternal optimist. I always think there's a way forward. I know there are opportunities waiting for someone to identify and grasp. I believe in the power of hard work. It's not going to be easy. Know that. And think about what level of success you're after. Do you want to stand out? Okay, great. Be prepared to work hard and make sacrifices. But you don't have to be top dog if you don't want to be. That's okay, too. You might be content with a less stressful level of success. It's up to you.

Whatever it is that you're after for your life and business, I would say that amid the turmoil of the world right now, the best thing to do is keep your composure. Stay calm. Dream. Plan. Focus. I know that never giving up is the foundation to success and reaching goals.

Starting at the age of twenty-one, I transformed a one-man, one-truck moving outfit into the biggest moving company in Canada, AMJ Campbell Van Lines, which at its peak twenty years later, had one thousand trucks on the road and boasted $125 million in annual revenue.

After an unhappy exit from the company I founded, I switched industries altogether and built Canada's largest extended-stay accommodations business, Premiere Executive Suites, which had more than twelve hundred furnished units and twenty offices across Canada.

Then I jumped back into the moving business—I told you the adventure was sometimes messy—by co-founding a new company, Premiere Van Lines, which I helped grow into a national van line. Along the way, I co-founded Premiere Mortgage Centre, then started Atlantic Signature

Mortgage & Loan, which my partners and I eventually sold to Credit Union Atlantic; I invested in real estate; started self-storage businesses, one of which, Premiere Self Storage, I sold for $13.5 million. We added Premiere Car Wash to our Premiere brand of services. I bought a money-losing resort, Oceanstone, transforming it into a top Nova Scotia tourism destination.

Those various businesses made me a five-time winner in *Atlantic Business Magazine*'s Top 50 CEO rankings. I met and befriended many top business people in Canada. I made millions.

Now, before you think that such success has gone to my head, I will add another funny story that Bernardine, known to family and friends as Bernie, loves to rib me about. In the mid-1990s, while driving home from Moncton, New Brunswick, she stopped at an antique store near Truro, Nova Scotia, where she found a table that she wanted to buy. But with no room in her car to transport it, she was not going to get it. As she exited the store, she spotted an AMJ Campbell truck at a nearby gas station. She gestured to the driver to wait, rushed over, and asked if he could take the table to Halifax in his load.

The driver gave her a gruff look of shock.

"My husband is Tim Moore," she explained sweetly.

The driver appeared unfazed. "Who the hell is Tim Moore?"

"The president of AMJ Campbell," she replied.

I don't know what she had to show him to prove her claim. This was before everyone owned a cellphone. Still somewhat dumbfounded, the driver agreed to take the table to the Halifax terminal, where we could arrange for a smaller truck to bring it to Chester.

The lesson is a good one. You're never as important as you think you are. Humility is a superpower, believe it or not. It's a significant part of effective leadership. Though you still also have to be tough at times. Remaining down-to-earth, not letting success (and lots of money) go to your head, is as crucial to effective leadership as making hard decisions.

I've experienced many highs of entrepreneurship: scaling up; financial riches; creating a brand culture with smart, dynamic employees and partners; mergers; and raising capital, among other things. And I'm the first to admit that I've lived through many lows. I've had my share of misfires and outright failures: facing debt; putting a big investment on the line; a money-losing investment in a nursing home; and an advance payments company that was a well-concealed Ponzi scheme. No path is straightforward.

This book contains my story, my advice, combined with some amusing tales of adventure and misadventure. Why do I write? I have some records to set straight. But mostly I write out of a sense of profound gratitude for the people I have worked alongside to make my businesses a success and for the opportunities that came my way. I also believe in setting my stories down for the next generation because in doing so they can become a blueprint. Although a lot in the world changes, some foundational tenets of business do not. For example, others can learn the how and the why of business, the intention, the hardship, and how the wealth that it created came into being.

My message is clear. While I maintain that entrepreneurs are born—not everyone welcomes risk or wants to work as hard as required—they are also honed through hardship, hunger, failure, collaboration, and resilience. I am not a perfect individual. But I *am* a perfect example of how anyone can achieve success.

I was going to be a priest. I kid you not.

Chapter 1

Praise Be to Your Work Ethic

Character cannot be developed in ease and quiet.
Only through experience of trial and suffering can the soul be strengthened, ambition inspired, and success achieved.

HELEN KELLER

AT THE START OF THE DECADE OF FREE LOVE, THE 1960s, I wore an itchy cassock—a long, black robe—with a sash around my waist and a stiff clerical collar. I had no sense of the sexual revolution under way. No taste for drugs and rock 'n' roll. I was eighteen. When in church, I was called "Father." All the seminarians were at St. Augustine's, an imposing five-storey brick building with a tall, narrow cupola, situated on the Scarborough Bluffs in Toronto. Founded in 1913, it was a reputable institution with a great sports program and academics. My parents were delighted that as the eldest of six children in our family I was undertaking this respected profession. The education and boarding were free.

Sixty-seven men in my class set out on a six-year course to become ordained priests: three years of philosophy followed by three years of theology. We had private rooms, which were small and utilitarian, with a sink and a toilet. There was a common shower. No one was allowed to visit others in their rooms. The only people who could come in were the priests. We rose at 5:00 each morning. An hour of praying in the chapel was followed by a simple breakfast of porridge and bread. The food was passable, but there was never enough of it. In all, we spent three hours a day in prayer in the chapel, which I remember as intimate and peaceful. For two afternoons a week we could leave the seminary. I would go home to Etobicoke, in Toronto's west end, or work for a charity. I remember travelling on a city bus and looking out the window at people just going about their daily lives. I felt removed from all that, sequestered I suppose. Did I feel a longing to join that world? I can't say for certain. I only know that I recognized I was not part of how most people lived.

I lasted three years in the seminary. I often joke about those years that I learned what it would be like to be locked up in jail. But I don't mean to disparage the experience. I think of it as part of my foundation. I enjoyed the daily ritual of prayer, the opportunity to express gratitude, deepen my understanding of Christian values, and to contemplate the afterlife. I have always held a deep spirituality. My wife, Bernardine, and I attend church most Sundays. And I pray every time I get on an airplane! Friendships among the seminarians were close and memorable. To this day, I recall them with great fondness. We played pranks on one another. Movies were screened every week. Endless games of Ping-Pong took up spare time. The studies were intense. It was like being in university. I enjoyed school for the first time. There was a strong sense of belonging and common purpose.

At the time, I really thought I was going to live my life as a priest. I worked hard to live up to the expectation. My family was Catholic. I grew up attending mass every Sunday. It was just what you did. And I had attended Michael Power High School in the Catholic school system in west-end Toronto, run by priests of the Oblates of Mary Immaculate order. In that era, priests were known to be extremely strict and severe. Some priests used yardsticks to whack students. In one incident, I had welts on my backside for two weeks. My infraction? Forgetting my French textbook two days in a row.

I tell you this because it doesn't matter where you start in life, how many false starts you may have had, or how well you did in school. I was miserable at academics in elementary and high school, having failed grades 3, 12, and 13, as I mentioned. Part of the problem was that I couldn't see the blackboard. No one checked my eyesight. And I was too embarrassed at the thought of wearing glasses, so I didn't say anything.

In grade 10, I dropped math. I felt that I didn't have the aptitude for academics or the will to concentrate. It wasn't that I was interested in girls either. (Well, that's not quite true. I did find the time in my final year of high school to meet and even propose to a Miss Toronto finalist. She said yes, but then quickly broke it off, which devastated me and amplified the self-esteem problem.) I wasn't the party type. In fact, I was shy. I lacked confidence, having severe acne that covered my face and body. In grade 11, I finally did get glasses, which didn't help my appearance.

People who know me in the business world will laugh at that admission. A guy who drove a red Rolls-Royce Corniche and wore burgundy cowboy boots with his Harry Rosen suits along with suspenders? *That guy is shy?* In truth, during those heady early days of business success in the mid-1980s, I was covering up my shyness. I did swagger around! In Allan Gould's 1986 book, *The New Entrepreneurs: 80 Canadian Success Stories,* in which he features founders, including Alex Tilley of Tilley hats, the Barish family of Dickie Dee ice cream, and Greig Clark of College

Pro Painters, among others, he describes me as "tall, dark, handsome, with Tom Selleck good looks and a mustache as thick as his bankroll." Gee, pretty good PR, don't you think? And I didn't even invite it. I had started in the moving industry and grown AMJ Campbell Van Lines into a national player. At that point, the company had thirteen branches in seven provinces from Halifax to Vancouver, nearly eight hundred employees, and more than $13 million in gross sales.

I was performing for Allan, no doubt about it, creating a persona of bold fearlessness. I wanted others to believe in me, even if I wasn't so sure of myself. Often, you must push yourself to appear as if you have confidence. I had struggled with a lack of it for many years. Certainly, as a pimply teenager the only thing I was good at was sports. I played basketball, football as running back, ran track, and competed in pole vault. The thought of catapulting myself 3.5 metres in the air with a steel pole—my personal best height—makes me wince now. I loved all those sports at the time.

My favourite, though, was basketball. Our team was the best in Toronto. I focussed my attention on winning, on beating my competitors, which may explain my later drive in the business world. Twice, I was voted top athlete in my school. In fact, I applied for a track and field scholarship to Cornell University in the United States, but didn't get in. (Hmm, I had an embarrassingly dreadful average, close to 35 percent upon graduation, which might explain the rejection!) I wasn't sure what to pursue. Not all of us know at that age. Some do. But not me. The priests at my high school suggested the seminary. They saw something in me, I suppose. And with encouragement, I wanted to please. I'm not even sure exactly what it was that drew me to that vocation. In part, I think I was attracted to the promise of stability. And I had a familiarity with discipline.

My upbringing at home had not been easy. I was born in Montréal in the mid-forties into a strict household that ran on a fifties-era style of parenting. My parents, Tom and June, had six children in quick succession: me, Lynn, Terry, Ted, Bonnie, and Anne. Unlike many of today's parents, who are child-centred, focussed on their offspring's self-esteem and success, my mother and father were too busy for one-on-one nurturing. It was a common approach to parenting in those days. They didn't show us outward signs of love; hugs were scarce. Nor did they offer support. I don't recall ever hearing either of my parents say, "Good job," "Nice work," or "We're proud of you." I was never encouraged to do better in school. My father never attended my sporting activities. Like any child, I craved affection, love, encouragement, and positivity. Not receiving that had an enormous impact on me. I didn't have a strong sense of self or faith in my abilities. That could explain my poor academic performance. I know now that I could have done better, much better. But at the time, I didn't see any evidence to suggest that I *could* do well.

Skiing was the only outdoor activity we did together as a family and the only pursuit we bonded over. My grandfather, Charles H. Moore, was a skiing pioneer who was profiled in H. P. Douglas's book *History of Skiing in Canada* (1951). My father passed that passion on to us, and we spent most of our winter weekends on hills around the Orangeville and Collingwood areas north of Toronto. Our Saturday tradition for many years involved skiing during the day, a family dinner, and then watching an NHL game together in the evening. We were even profiled in the defunct *Toronto Telegram Weekend Magazine*, in March 1962, when I was seventeen. The article ran under the headline: "Skiing for Eight—on a Budget." The subheading read: "Fun-filled winter weekends are a way of life for the Moore family." There was a photo of the eight of us standing in a line on a hill, looking ready to race each other to the bottom. Underneath the photo was the following cutline: "By budgeting wisely, the family keeps the costs down to about $15 for a weekend at Hockley Valley, 40 miles north of their home in suburban Toronto." It still amazes me that a family could ski for a weekend on just $15. All six Moore kids went on to be certified ski instructors. My brother, Terry, who later went into business with me, now teaches skiing three days a week in his retirement.

The part of that newspaper story about our family ski trips that makes me laugh is the praise of my family for budgeting wisely. Budgets? Wise financial discipline? That was the last thing you could say about my father. Money was a huge problem in our family. I will go so far as to say the experience of living with financial stress as a child scarred me for life—but, here's the kicker, it was in a good way! Certainly, good for my business life. I was extremely focussed on expenditure and debt from the start of my career as an entrepreneur.

Everyone is shaped by their upbringing. When I'm interviewing someone for a job or to bring on as a partner, I always ask about their background. By observing someone, you can often gain insight into what their childhood was like. It's important insight in terms of being able to build trust and understand the character of an employee or partner. The most important thing for anyone is to gain perspective on your own childhood and how it affected you. I think of it as learning to decode yourself. If you see the influence of your childhood with clarity, you can acknowledge it, act on it, fix it, and, if needed, transcend it. You can know yourself in a full way, which allows you to unblock yourself if you feel stuck. For me, my family shaped me in three profound ways.

One was my lifelong love of sports. I have remained active and athletic throughout my life. I have had a few health scares, but I always bounce back because of my commitment to physical fitness. Even during the busiest periods of my business career, I always made time for exercise: running, weightlifting, skiing.

Another was my relationship to money. My father was an overly harsh man. He was overbearing in many ways. He was also a dreamer, a salesman who was well liked by his clients, but who lived far beyond his means. He worked in the material handling equipment business, selling items like dollies and forklifts, anything that was needed in warehouse-based companies. He worked hard and he hustled. I'll give him that. I guess you could say he was a wheeler-dealer type of character. But he never paid his bills on time. He was not a good businessman. Creditors harangued us on the phone. My mother never had any money. Household expenses were tightly controlled. At times, there were horrible arguments about money.

But from the outside, you'd never know we were in debt. We had a nice house in Thorncrest Village, a neighbourhood of tree-lined winding streets that had been designed by architect and town planner Eugene Faludi as Toronto's first modern suburb in 1945. We had a farm in Barrie, one hour north of Toronto. We had a cottage in the Laurentians in Quebec for skiing. My father cruised about town in a shiny Cadillac. He never sought financial advice. Sadly, he was forced into bankruptcy twice.

The third influence was work ethic. In our family, it was drummed into us from an early age. My first job was at age ten as a newspaper delivery boy. My father marched into my bedroom early on a Saturday morning, yanking the blankets off me. "Get up!" he ordered. "It's time to get to work." As the eldest, I was an example to my siblings and put under severe stress to work hard. My father was always pushing me to do more.

"You have to get out and work and pay your own way," my father insisted. Pound the pavement was his advice for getting work. At age eleven, I started working in a Toronto smoke shop. For sixty cents an hour, I worked behind the counter, scooped ice cream, hauled boxes of soda up from the basement. I did whatever was asked of me. As a kid, it was terrific to earn my own money, even though it wasn't very much. I learned that I had some agency.

Another of my early jobs in Toronto was running a donut wagon on Saturday mornings. Similar to a milk delivery service, we'd roll along suburban streets, and I'd sprint up and down house and apartment stairs, delivering donuts and milk from a wagon. A morning's work earned me a couple of dollars and some free donuts.

Later in my teenage years, I spent two summers loading boxcars for CN. I had an obsession about working hard. It was known among the crew that if they worked with me, they would finish early for the day. During my third summer with the railway, when I was eighteen, I spent part of it on a "chain gang," comprised mainly of Italian and Portuguese immigrants. Our job was to lay tracks in the bug-swarming forests of Northern Ontario. Not fun. We rose every day at 5:00 A.M., worked long days in the oppressive heat, bathed in lakes, and slept in boxcars. All for a dollar an hour! It was rough work and often dangerous, especially *after* our shifts ended. Whenever we hit a small town, some of the workers would drink heavily and get into bar brawls. During one fight someone pulled a knife, resulting in the CN police arriving to sort it out. I phoned my parents shortly after, which put an end to that summer experience. They agreed that I should immediately come home.

By the end of high school, I had worked about twenty different jobs. Once in Montréal, while working at the La Ronde amusement park, I worked so hard I ended up in hospital, suffering from exhaustion. I had a nosebleed that wouldn't stop. I was working twenty hours a day on double shifts.

But I don't regret that discipline. It accounts for much of my success. The desire to work hard is not something you can teach. It's like curiosity. You either have it or you don't. And if you have the desire to put your nose to the grindstone, to burn the midnight oil, pat yourself on the back and celebrate. Indulge that impulse. It's a beautiful thing to be self-sufficient, to know that you can always find your way, make your own money, and create opportunities. There is something to be said for work-life balance, which I admit I had to learn, but I am proudly a somewhat recovering workaholic. For the first twenty years of my career, I worked seven days a week. I don't think there is any successful entrepreneur who isn't a hard worker.

So why did I quit the seminary? Out of that class of sixty-seven men, only about five stuck with it and became priests. Some were expelled for homosexuality. I didn't even know what being gay was about. The only hint of unwelcome affection from a priest at the seminary was a hug that felt like it went on too long and made me uncomfortable.

The reason I left was a girl.

During Expo 67 in Montréal, I got a job in the games area of La Ronde, an amusement park that was part of the celebrated complex of international pavilions commemorating Canada's one hundredth anniversary. Tourists came in droves. And there I was, manning one of the kiosks where you pay to try your luck at tossing balls into baskets or knocking over pins. A perfect way to meet people. Soon enough, I met a beautiful girl, Barbara, who was visiting from Colorado with her parents. I took her out for a soda. I appreciated the fact that she was religious. She attended a Christian college. Our views on life were similar, and we communicated through writing letters after the summer. She came back to Canada for Christmas. I should add that in the seminary, some of my friends and I talked often about the desire to marry. We thought the church would relax their rules. Maybe that was just our interpretation. I can't be sure. The majority of the Catholic Church still follows the rule of clerical celibacy. Only some sects in the Eastern Catholic Church allow priests to marry.

After that Christmas, I didn't go back to seminary. Barb didn't return to Christian college. Instead, we married in a courthouse.

My parents were embarrassed that I had quit the seminary. They essentially disowned me. For three years, they would not communicate with me.

During those years of silence from my parents, Barbara and I moved to Sudbury, Ontario, where I got a job teaching grades 7 and 8. I did that for a year and a half. While that choice of vocation may seem like another puzzling change of direction, I see the through line. I'd always wanted to teach or coach sports. That stint in Sudbury was one of the best experiences of my life. I felt that I was making an impact, and most of the kids were pleasant to teach. I was also making $4,000 a year, big money for me. As the only male teacher in the school, I often had to be the disciplinarian, a role the priests had prepared me well for. But I was a kind disciplinarian. I truly cared about the students and spent a great deal of time with the most troubled ones. Having grown up in challenging circumstances myself, I felt a connection to them and believed I could reach them more readily than some of the other teachers. Maybe that was the seminarian in me: wanting to offer the kids appreciation and understanding. There was a common denominator to my character after all.

I had been given the job at the high school in Sudbury with a "letter of permission" from the education department. To carry on with a teaching career, I would need a university degree. Barbara and I moved to Waterloo, Ontario, and I enrolled in Wilfrid Laurier University, then known as Waterloo Lutheran University. I threw myself into my studies. I even took on an academic persona, sporting a beard and a tweed jacket and smoking a pipe. It was all or nothing with me. I loved to have long philosophical discussions with some of the professors. Despite my atrocious academic track record, I graduated with an honours degree in history in 1970.

But that scholastic success contrasted with the failure of my marriage. Barbara and I had two boys, Jason and Timmy, one after the other. We were both young, immature, and set in our ways. We had married in haste. We were living separate lives. I was deeply ensconced in the academic life while taking part-time jobs to support the family. She belonged to a strict evangelical church with restrictions on alcohol, dancing, smoking, and other activities that most people take for granted. With Barb, there was no compromise. I came home once with a case of beer, and she went through the roof in anger and disappointment. She locked me out of the house. It wasn't going to work. After three years, we split up, giving me the inglorious honour of being the first in my family to divorce. I remain grateful to Barb for our two talented sons, who have big hearts and good souls.

After we dissolved the marriage, Barb and the boys departed for Colorado, while I headed back to Montréal. This was where I'd grown up, so it felt like the right place to go to regroup. When people ask me about setbacks, personal or professional, my response is always that you must never lose hope. No matter how disappointing a turn of event is, move on. Life has a way of throwing curve balls at you—some are terrific and some are difficult. Something new is always around the corner, whether that's a piece of business after losing a client; a new opportunity in employment or starting a business; meeting a new person; living somewhere different. That's the lesson. Life is abundant. Push forward and prepare for the next surprise.

When I arrived in Montréal, I was full of vim to get ahead and make my way—again. I enrolled at McGill University, aiming to get a master's degree in history. To this day, I remain one course and a thesis short of that degree.

But another shift in my life was about to happen.

While at McGill, I was broke. So I was working a side hustle to make money. A friend of mine in Waterloo had told me how much he was making per day as a mover. I was stunned. *I'm strong, I can haul boxes and furniture, I can drive a van*, I thought to myself.

That job soon became a full-time career, forcing me to quit McGill. It was the doorway to becoming a millionaire many times over. My life was changing direction again.

It started with a second-hand pickup truck.

Chapter 2

Understand Your Business from the Ground Up

Adaptability is the simple secret of survival.

JESSICA HAGEDORN

American author, playwright, poet, and performance artist

I COULDN'T HAVE ANTICIPATED THE BROOM LADY, THAT'S for sure. It was January 1971, and I was a complete neophyte in the moving business. I didn't know what to expect. I had traded in my little Volkswagen for a $2,000 Ford pickup. I installed steel bars and wooden slats on the sides and back of the second-hand truck. Then I affixed a frame over the bed and draped a protective tarp overtop. Those rough modifications, which basically created a 2.5-metre-long box covered by a tarp, allowed me to move the contents of a one-bedroom apartment in a single trip. Moore Moving was in business with its first truck, serving the city of Montréal.

I placed ads in community newspapers, including the *NDG Monitor*, *The McGill Daily*, and *The Westmount Examiner*, offering my services for seven dollars an hour.

MAKE ONE "MOORE" MOVE

THEN COMPARE—WE CARE

RELIABLE STUDENT MOVERS

LOW RATES

I liked the simplicity of the job—or what I perceived as its simplicity. You have a truck, a dolly, some straps and winches. You pack, lift, heave, load, drive, unload, and unpack. Seems simple, right? A job not requiring much except physical strength. And the best part: a fistful of cash—and a cold beer—at the end of a moving day. A tangible result and a feeling of accomplishment—not bad. But while much of what I describe as the physical aspect of the job is true—"all brawn and no brain," as I once quipped about the popular perception of the industry—it is far more complex than it first appears.

Hence, my story about the Broom Lady.

It was my very first moving job. A woman called requesting a quick apartment move of seven or eight boxes. *Great*, I thought. *An easy gig.* I figured it would take an hour of my time, so I quoted her my hourly rate of seven dollars.

But the job unfolded like something out of a comedic slapstick routine. Laurel and Hardy come to mind. I arrived at her building, all eager and bright-eyed. Earnest, too. An attendant told me to proceed to the underground parking where I could load my truck.

"No problem," I replied, thanking him and waving from my open window. I drove down the ramp leading to the underground section.

CRUNCH.

The entrance had a two-metre clearance. I hadn't paid attention to the sign. And in my excitement over my first job, I forgot the height of my modified moving truck: more than three metres in the back, thanks to the box I'd installed over the bed. I leapt out of my truck to discover I had damaged my contraption and ripped the tarp. All before I had moved a single box for my first customer.

I backed my damaged truck out of the parkade, feeling foolish. But never mind. I arrived at her apartment with a big smile. She showed me two or three rooms full of boxes and furniture. This was not a quick job!

"Everything is going?" I asked politely.

"Of course," she replied.

"I thought you only had seven or eight boxes," I noted.

"Everything must go!" she exclaimed, clearly unaware that she had misrepresented the job—or was unwilling to admit that she had misrepresented it on purpose. Who knows?

I showed no hesitation, wanting to do as I had promised. I hauled her boxes, one after the other, into my sad-looking truck.

Then she asked if I could drive her to the new apartment while delivering the truckload.

"Of course," I replied. Was I pleased that I had also managed to become a taxi service as well? No! But what can you do? I wanted to please my customer.

During the journey with her in the passenger seat, I diplomatically pointed out that the seven-dollar fee didn't compensate me fairly for the work I'd done and that I'd have to charge more.

But sympathy was not the Broom Lady's strong suit. She quickly swivelled in her seat to look me straight in the eye and pronounced that she would hold me to my quote and not pay a cent more.

I suppressed my anger, vowing silently that I'd never make the same mistake again.

That first move was a disaster. Financially, it was a loss, what with gas and my time. Apart from my days laying track for CN, it was the hardest I've ever worked for seven dollars. It took me five hours to cram the contents of her apartment into my truck and move everything to the new destination.

But I remained polite and wished her well.

Three months later, she called again. I accepted the job after she agreed to pay by the hour—no matter how long it took—and at my new rate of nine dollars. She agreed.

I was building the business and needing the money. And I was determined to be smarter in my second dealing with this prickly customer. This time, she was headed to Europe and needed her entire apartment moved to her parents' house for storage. I completed the move on a Friday. The next evening, I was sitting in my apartment when the woman called in a panic.

"Tim, you forgot my broom! Why didn't you move my broom?"

I was confused. "What broom?" I asked. "I didn't see a broom."

She was incensed. "The broom behind the door. There was a broom behind the door. I need my broom!" *Yeah,* I thought to myself, *you need your broom to fly yourself around and scare the living daylights out of your friends—if you have friends, that is.*

I maintained my composure and suggested that she should have made the broom visible to us. She was there during the move. Clients often supervise a move. But no. She would hear none of my defence. Did I want to drive across town, retrieve a broom, and take it to her on a Saturday night, while having a drink and watching a hockey game?

That broom needed to be brought to her immediately, she insisted. Not tomorrow. Not when I had time. She even threatened to report me to the Better Business Bureau or the local newspaper if I didn't do her bidding. Still no sympathy. Still no compromise on what she considered our iron-clad deal.

So, what did I do? I went to get that broom and delivered it to her where she waited at her parents' house. That broom probably cost a dollar to buy new. But the cost to me of driving all over town to get it for her was close to fifteen dollars. I like to imagine the Broom Lady flying around on her bloody broom in a pointy witch hat to match her crotchety attitude.

She and her broom certainly flew directly into hilarious company lore, told countless times. Several years later, when I was running AMJ Campbell moving company—then a large multi-million-dollar business—we hired former NHL agitator Eddie Shack to deliver a keynote speech at one of our client appreciation events. Shack was a charismatic speaker, a great draw and entertaining. But he loved to swear. I was a bit concerned that his style wouldn't be to everyone's liking. As our event approached, my fears increased when I heard that Shack had recently uttered crude language in front of a crowd that included a priest and young children. So before our event, which was fully booked with four hundred people, I called his agent and informed him that his star speaker needed to watch his language. I couldn't risk offending important clients. No problem, the agent assured me.

On the night of the event, I opened the proceedings as I always did with a few comments and stories, including the one about the Broom Lady. (I had made her famous! Famous and anonymous. If only she knew!) Then I introduced Eddie. Having heard my story about my difficult customer, he wasted no time in telling the crowd exactly where he would have put the woman's broom.

I was mortified! But the crowd roared with laughter. It was a line only Eddie Shack could deliver.

Ironically, despite my frustrations with the Broom Lady, she taught me many things that set me up for success in my business. I learned that you have to know your business from the bottom up. Get into the trenches of your business and pay attention. The dynamics of a successful business begin at ground level. Who are your front-line workers? What must they do well? What personality type do they need to be? What is reasonable to ask of them in a workday? Who is the customer? What do they want? What do they need?

And remember this: the customer is always right. It's almost a cliché, but clichés exist for a reason. They're true.

In the beginning, I was a softie. A pushover. With my background in teaching and three years spent in a seminary, I was unprepared for business ownership. There were all kinds of situations where I made very little money. I was in survival mode.

My company was a ragtag operation, run out of whatever apartment I was living in at the time: first, a dingy fifteen-dollar-per-week basement unit, then a one-bedroom on Montréal's De Maisonneuve Boulevard. I served as chief mover, dispatcher, and sales manager. I had a small desk and a phone—and a little trick to help me manage. I called it my Voice Modulation Technique. I always answered the phone in a deep and serious voice since I never knew who I was dealing with. If it was someone who had a problem or was being difficult, I would maintain my authoritarian don't-mess-with-me voice. But if the caller was simply inquiring about a move and opened up about their needs or a claim for damage,

I could easily switch to my nice guy voice. I wanted to be the friendly mover in that instance.

It was crucial that I develop an inner toughness and a well-considered leadership philosophy. I learned pretty quickly that the moving business can be rough. It's a trucking business, essentially. Serious problems arise. Not everybody is nice. And there were thousands of times when I would find myself exhausted, wondering why I was doing it. Like the time I was in a blinding snowstorm in Montréal at midnight, the wind blowing the tarp off the back of my truck. I had to get out there to fasten it down, frozen as an Arctic explorer, battling the snow whipping around me. Or the time one of my drivers called in a panic to tell me they had loaded a truck with boxes and furniture, but they hadn't tied it down. And guess what? They were parked on an incline, a sharp incline, and all the furniture and boxes...yup, started to tumble out the back onto the driveway.

But one thing I never changed is my strong belief that you must treat people with respect. Always. In my experience, 90 percent of companies don't understand what real service truly is. For me, in those early years in the moving business my greatest asset was my attitude. It led to referrals by word of mouth. Referrals are the lifeblood of any business. As it turned out, advertising wasn't necessary. I didn't even list my company in the *Yellow Pages* until 1977, and that was *the* way to get your name out there. New business was constantly flooding in.

I made it my goal to become familiar with different ethnic communities in Montréal so I could understand what they needed and what mattered to them. I was always investigating ways to reach new markets and get more business. I enjoyed the opportunity to learn about other people.

I worked like a dog, though. At the end of my first week in business, I made $300 in cash. Always cash. It was easy to make money, and it felt good. Some people wouldn't pay their bills—another nuisance in running your own company. But I was adamant about getting paid. Once, at two in the morning, I drove to a customer's dwelling and demanded the money they owed me. Movers had just finished the job. I told them to stay until I got there. The customers weren't going to pay because of a minor issue. I politely explained that I needed payment. Which they coughed up, somewhat sleepily!

I always kept my price very competitive. I never consciously undercut other companies on price, though I knew I was well below them. I worked hard, and I was fair. I wasn't going to let someone get away with not paying me.

My prices reflected my lack of overhead. And I maximized revenue by rounding up to the nearest half hour. I was flying by the seat of my jeans! I used my small vehicle to my advantage when making my pitch to potential clients—even clients looking to move five-bedroom houses. Yes, I would have to make multiple trips, but I wouldn't have to spend time carefully loading a large moving van, where items need to be packed perfectly and strapped down. My pickup could be loaded and unloaded easily, so each trip would be quick. It was simple: load quickly, drive, unload quickly, return. Using that strategy, moving the contents of a four- or five-bedroom house was no issue for me, provided that the distance between the two points was short—perhaps three or four kilometres.

I studied and anticipated the busy and slow periods of the marketplace. On May 1, half the city of Montréal, it seemed, was moving to a new home, as that was the date many apartment rental leases terminated. I hired students, sometimes as many as thirty, employed at $2/hour and billed at $9/hour. Everyone likes to help students, so this arrangement built a good community-focussed reputation as well. I worked seven days a week, twenty hours a day, double shifts, triple shifts. Whatever it took. Eventually, I could make $20,000 in four days.

I was creative. I moved garbage when there was a garbage strike. Once, I drove a lady's sister and her cat to Ottawa from Montréal. (That involved stopping every half hour for the cat to pee!) But they paid my hourly rate, so I didn't mind. On the subject of cats, one customer who was moving from Calgary to Winnipeg lost their cat, only to find her when we unloaded the truck—alive! A good story.

One move required getting a washing machine out of the basement of an old Montréal house, a task that could only be achieved by removing some of the basement stairs. I didn't know anything about removing stairs, but I worked my way through it.

Let me be clear: I still made mistakes. One customer called for a quote on a cross-border job: moving two-and-a-half rooms of furniture from Boston to Montréal. I told him I'd do it for $45. (Other companies would have charged $300.) He would pay for the gas. A 1,000-kilometre roundtrip that should have taken twelve hours morphed into a twenty-four-hour winter nightmare through a snowstorm. It was a hard-won lesson in pricing. It's one thing to beat your competitors on price, but you won't survive by also defeating yourself in the process. Your pricing must be fair *and* profitable *and* sustainable.

I took risks. I didn't have insurance. For the first three years, I didn't keep accounting books. I paid no taxes. I didn't have time to do the accounting, and I had little financial know-how.

And I didn't have a cartage licence, which is expensive. Interprovincial cartage licences were even more, close to $5,000, well beyond my means at the time. The specific licensing requirements vary depending on the type and weight of the vehicle, as well as the nature of the cargo being transported. To avoid commercial weigh stations along major highways, I drove my truck during the night for out-of-province moves. I was the Midnight Trucker, which sounds like the title of a movie. Maybe a comedic drama?

My brother Terry often came to help. During one move from Montréal to Toronto, he was driving my half-ton truck with the back fully loaded, a mattress strapped to the top, and the customer hitching a ride beside him. He didn't have an interprovincial licence. Outside Kingston, Ontario, the mattress flew off the roof and landed in the road. Terry wasn't even aware it had come off. Within minutes, a police car was approaching, lights flashing, bearing the mattress on top of the cruiser. Terry was petrified. What if they asked to see his permit? The officer in the passenger seat had his hand out the window of the police car, gripping the side of the mattress. Terry pulled over. The police officers never asked for a permit. Assuming Terry was moving his own stuff, they helped him strap the mattress back on the roof. Close call!

Oh, yes. I was doing what I had to do to make a buck. No apologies. No regrets.

By the end of the first year, I'd made $10,000. I was careful with the money, thanks to my childhood experiences. Three months into my moving venture, I bought a second truck. After two years in business, I bought my first big twenty-four-foot truck, a purchase that gave me a profound sense of accomplishment. I changed my company name from Moore Moving to TC Moore Transport. I was starting to build a brand because I had examined the industry to see how I could be different.

That's the trick to entrepreneurialism. If you're launching a start-up with a brand-new product, that's one thing. But if you're running a business that has many competitors, you must decipher what makes you stand out.

One of the ways I differentiated my company was my insistence that all workers wear red T-shirts emblazoned with the TC Moore logo and company name. This was a unique approach because movers often looked—and often still do look—dishevelled and rough. I wanted to portray a sense of neatness, order, and professionalism. My workers were all clean-cut and identically dressed.

I was driven to make money and be successful. During those early years, I dabbled in several other small businesses to make extra cash between moves or during slow periods. One was carpet cleaning. (I ended up turning someone's white shag rug into an ugly yellow hue.) Another was house painting. (A fear of heights didn't help that business venture.) I got involved in promoting Pong games in bars. All these ventures were short-lived.

It can take time to find your groove. Experiment. Dabble. Test the waters.

I have a name for that early period of my life as an entrepreneur: My Lunatic Years.

When I say that you must understand your business from the ground up, I mean not only that you have to appreciate the job of the person at the lowest rung of the company—like the driver or the receptionist—but you also have to develop the emotional intelligence to know your customer.

A move is traumatic. It's right up there with divorce, a death in the family, and bankruptcy.

David Way, a long-time AMJ Campbell employee and later a franchise owner, summarized it like this: "Moving isn't like manufacturing. It can be volatile. Bad weather, delayed house closings, closed roads, traffic, and so many other things have an impact on how we perform our jobs. A lot of things are really outside our control, but customers don't always see it that way. Moving makes even the most rational people unreasonable at times. It certainly makes for an interesting (if sometimes frustrating) work environment. Customer emotions run high and, basically, we work with nothing more sophisticated than 'men and machines,' at least on the physical side of moving."

The moving sector brings you into people's lives. Our homes are our world. When you enter someone's house, you see who they are by how they live. You see what their sense of taste is. If they're tidy or messy. If they're rich or middle class. By moving them to a new location, you can tell if they're doing well or struggling, moving up or down in the world. Relocations often happen at hinge moments in people's lives: marriage, a growing family, divorce, job loss, a newly empty nest, aging issues, widowhood. It's no wonder moves are traumatic.

One episode remains clear in my memory. I was hired to move the belongings of a seemingly refined, cultured McGill professor. I expected boxes of books and a stately wooden desk to be among his possessions. Instead, I discovered a hovel with cheap furniture and a chesterfield crawling with fleas and maggots. I'm not sure what had happened in his life to precipitate the move, but something was afoot. He explained that it was his dog's chesterfield, but I didn't care whose it was. It was disgusting. I moved him of course, and right after, went home for a shower.

You have a clear view of people's personality once inside their door. One of my salesmen once showed up for an appointment to estimate the cost of a move to find the owner wearing a negligee when she answered the door. When she took him through her house to assess the quantity of contents, there were nude portraits of her everywhere. Apparently, she was a nude model. We didn't get her business. She certainly was memorable!

I also came to appreciate the importance of belongings. Furniture. We think of it as inanimate, just objects. But for most people, their belongings carry a lot of emotional significance. Think of the unfortunate people who have lost a home in a wildfire. The collection of memories is often the collection of furniture, art, tchotchkes. That dining-room table is where people gathered for birthdays and holidays. Maybe it was handed down by a beloved grandmother. A chair may have been where a mother nurtured her newborn.

So, of course, as movers we must respect these things our clients treasure. (It also explains the trauma from damage to belongings, when it happens, and the importance of dealing with claims in a professional manner.)

I remember one lady following me down the stairs from her apartment as I carried a table. "Careful, careful," she kept repeating to me as though that table were a young child. In the context of her overprotectiveness, the thought briefly crossed my mind that the scenario would be a great Candid Camera moment: I would drop the piece of furniture and listen to the crash and watch the expression on my client's face. She was obsessed with this table. "Careful, careful," she continued as I took it up the ramp into the back of my truck, wrapping it with care in a thick blanket and strapping it down. It's a wonder she didn't kiss that table and wish it a good and safe journey to its new home.

I assured her of my respect for her belongings. I truly felt it. I empathized with my customers. I wanted to be helpful. Simply put, if you're not committed to excellent customer service, then the service industry isn't for you.

My enthusiasm for this topic was perhaps best captured in an *Atlantic Progress* magazine article from 1998, which ran under the headline, "Tim Moore Takes the Trauma Out of Moving." We identified people who would find moving especially difficult—such as seniors—and leveraged our reputation for care and good service. We offered discounts for members of the Canadian Association of Retired Persons (CARP), for example.

It's hard to be truly successful with a venture if you don't genuinely *like* the business. I liked how we could make a difference in people's lives. I liked how we could build a memorable brand and offer extras that other moving companies didn't. Furthermore, building and expanding a business is much easier if you can have fun doing it.

Throughout my career, I've given countless lectures to students in high school, college, and university. Their optimism and curiosity are contagious. My central message has always been this: If you want to make money—*real* money—consider entrepreneurship. Or instill a sense of entrepreneurship in the business in which you're working. Think about how to innovate, how to expand. Significant financial wealth can be obtained in various professions, but only entrepreneurial businesses allow you to amass wealth while also creating and building something yourself. Plus, you gain the security and independence that comes with constructing something of your own—a business you hold equity in, perhaps even 100 percent ownership.

Entrepreneurship offers the opportunity for riches and deep satisfaction. You must work tenaciously and accept levels of stress and risk that others can't tolerate. In my experience, however, the payoff is more than worth the effort and stress.

By 1974, I had a fleet of five trucks, which were always on the go, often seven days a week. Toward the end of the 1970s, after eight years in the business, I had achieved some significant success. My confidence was growing. I'd amassed close to $100,000 in equity.

But another twist in my tale lay ahead.

I was feeling a little burnt out from endless hours of driving, hauling, running dispatch, dealing with claims, and handling sales. And I still felt a pull toward teaching. After receiving an offer to teach elementary school in Peel County, west of Toronto, I decided to sell TC Moore Transport to two of my employees for $80,000. (Unfortunately, the company later joined Mayflower Transit, a competitor, and went bankrupt.)

There was another reason. It was a girl—again.

I first saw Bernardine Mary Bohan, a pretty teacher from Moncton, New Brunswick, at a party in Montréal. I watched her from across the room. She was slim with a small stature. Her brown hair reached to her shoulders. Her eyes were sparkly and kind. She was quick to smile. I don't remember what she was wearing. I thought I caught her looking my way a couple of times. Whether it was my long hair, my moustache, my ugly orange silk shirt—she remembered that!—or the fact that I was a truck driver, something must have appealed to her.

"I'd love to get your phone number," I said, sidling up to her and engaging her in conversation. (I was good with people, as I've said.) She obliged and I memorized her number on the spot. I called her the next day.

In 1977, we were engaged with plans to get married that May. It didn't seem wise to launch into marriage—for a second time—while running a small moving company that required my 24-7 attention. I would go back to teaching, a profession we both loved and thought we could share.

Or so I thought.

A call from my accountant changed everything—again.

Chapter 3

Fear Is Your Warrior Emotion

> The iron rule of life is: Everybody struggles. You have to soldier through it.... You can cry.... But you can't quit.
>
> **CHARLIE MUNGER**
> Vice-chair of Berkshire Hathaway

THERE IS LIFE *BEFORE* YOU MAKE A BIG DECISION AND life *after*. All entrepreneurs arrive at consequential inflection points. Invariably, that decision involves risk—and sometimes fear. Correction: It almost always involves fear. And so it should. You're often taking a big risk.

But fear is a wonderful motivator. It's an underrated emotion. We try to avoid it because we're conditioned to think of it as destructive. It can be, of course. But for an entrepreneur, it's par for the course. So, my advice? Think of it as the warrior emotion. As someone once said to me: You know you're not growing as a person or as a business person if you don't feel scared.

This wild and wonderful chapter of my career began when my accountant, Rick Renaud, called me with a question about my decision to give up the moving business after selling TC Moore Transport. I had hired him a few years before to do a little magic: namely, pull together a tax return out of thin air. Too busy running the business, I had kept very limited receipts. But by the end of the 1970s, people advised me to get my corporate financial house in order.

Rick was a little nerdy and very smart, rather low-key. I listened to him. I was working on improving my financial literacy, which was still very poor.

Rick liked what I had done at TC Moore Transport. I had "money anxiety"—staying out of debt and thinking carefully about my pricing—which can be attributed to my experience witnessing my father's financial struggles. Music to the ears of accountants. Rick appreciated my work ethic and ability to get business and follow up with potential customers.

"Why go back to teaching?" he asked me, clearly thinking I was nuts to consider it. A teacher didn't earn much income.

"I have an idea," he said. "Let's acquire a moving company, improve it, and flip it. Make a nice profit. In and out in maybe three years max."

I hesitated. But Rick's plan sounded straightforward. I was young. I could always go back to teaching in the years ahead, I reasoned. I consulted with Bernardine, who had worked with me at TC Moore Transport, handling the phone and sales. She trusted my judgment. We were in love and happy to take on an adventure together.

Rick had a great eye for spotting an opportunity. Before long, he identified MJ Campbell Moving and Storage, a forty-year-old company in Toronto and Barrie, a satellite city an hour north, that had mediocre operations, generating roughly $200,000 in annual revenue, five or six trucks, and a couple of leased warehouses. It also contained a few prizes. They were an agent for North American Van Lines, an internationally renowned organization. And they had provincial permits to move between Toronto and Barrie. Not only that, they had a rare permit allowing moves anywhere in Ontario as well as out West. This was huge.

MJ Campbell was also one of only three companies cleared to move soldiers to and from Camp Borden (now CFB Borden), the large training base located southwest of Barrie. This, too, was huge. It meant that MJ Campbell had access to valuable federal government business, which typically involved up to three hundred moves a year.

Rick had done his research well.

The only drawback was that by buying MJ Campbell, we would inherit the Teamsters Canada union. I am not a fan of unions. I don't like anyone telling me how to run my business. They can close you down. And if you have a bad employee, you can't get rid of them. I want to decide what my company *can* pay its employees; I won't have a union dictating what it believes I *should* pay my employees. I knew how to treat people well. I was confident in my approach and always worked in such a way that my employees would never feel the need to agitate for a union. My approach has been to promote an entrepreneurial spirit with financial incentives that reward strong workers and go-getters, employees who provide great service and generate new business for the company. Unions don't think that way.

Still, I decided to buy the company with Rick. I will tell you later how I dealt with the Teamsters union—and how it actually benefitted me in one instance. There are upsides to everything!

Shortly before Christmas 1977, Rick and I each paid $25,000 for the company. I was thirty-two years old and scared out of my wits. But I worked hard to push down that fear, looking for ways to build the business. I hired a terrific corporate sales wiz, Ron Stone, whom I poached from North American Van Lines, where he had been a senior executive.

Within a year we'd pushed sales to $350,000. We expanded into Montréal, Calgary, Edmonton, and Vancouver. I remained in Montréal during this time, commuting to and from Toronto each week, and often driving trucks when we were short on labour.

Once again, I was working seventy-five hours a week. The logistics were increasing in complexity, as were the financials of a multi-city company. I relegated all the accounting to Rick. That was how we divided our responsibilities. I ran the company. He ran the financials from Montréal.

By 1981, three years into the partnership, sales were $3 million. But I began to feel that Rick and I weren't working well together. A solid and well-balanced partnership can often help you grow a business more quickly than you could have done alone. Sometimes, though, the price of partnership can be higher than you expected.

I knew that Rick was what you might call a "creative" accountant. After all, he had magically produced my first tax return for TC Moore Transport with few receipts. But financial creativity can also be problematic. I didn't like some of his financial dealings once I discovered them. For one thing, he was using debt to cover our receivables in what became a never-ending financial juggling act. By 1981, we had maxed out our $400,000 line of credit. At one point, Rick and I both agreed to personally guarantee $25,000 of the company's debt. Later, I learned that he had secretly pulled out of the agreement, leaving me far more exposed than he was. Not good. I feared that this fiscal house of cards might soon collapse.

Not only that, Rick was also working a fraction of the hours I was for the same pay. And have I underscored often enough how hard I was working?

This “flip-job” had gone far enough, I decided. It was time to cash out. After some discussions, it was agreed that Rick would buy me out for $400,000.

That mindset would change when I asked for advice during lunch with an accountant from Clarkson Gordon. We met a couple of weeks before the deal with Rick to buy me out was scheduled to close. I was aware that my financial know-how was not the greatest, so I made it a habit to seek out different opinions on big decisions in order to weigh the pros and cons.

“Why on earth are you getting out?” I recall this other accountant saying. “You love this business! You’re good at it! Why give it all up?” It was true. I had a strong emotional attachment to it.

“I don’t want a dispute with Rick,” I explained without expanding on my disgruntled feelings about his financial dealings. “If I can get $400,000, that’s fine. I’ll be out. I’ll go do something else.”

The accountant shook his head. “I don’t know. I’m not sure you’re doing the right thing,” he replied.

That comment caused me to reconsider all that I was signing away: hundreds of thousands of dollars in earnings and ownership of a company that I’d built. I decided to seek out even more advice. The accountant connected me with a lawyer, Michel St. Pierre, who specialized in negotiations. He helped me analyze and think about the paperwork Rick had drawn up.

The deal had always been slightly lopsided in Rick’s favour. A few weeks later, when all of us met at the offices of Rick’s lawyer, his side tried to squeeze a bit harder and make changes to the deal. These new demands irked me. I now felt like I was getting screwed; not a nice feeling. Michel thought so, too. He called for a recess.

He and I withdrew to a private room where we discussed the deal that was now on the table.

"It's bad for you. I wouldn't do it," Michel advised.

He paused for a moment or two. Then, he looked at me and asked a question I never expected. "Would you accept the deal if it were reversed?"

I was surprised, but I could also see the merit of the deal if I were the one left owning the business. "Of course," I said.

We talked some more. A shrewd turntable tactic was about to be played out.

Back in the conference room, Michel looked down at the sale document, then pinned Rick with his eagle-eyed gaze.

"If you were Mr. Moore, would you accept these terms?" he asked nonchalantly.

"I would," Rick replied, telegraphing confidence that his proposal was more than fair.

Michel delayed his next move, adding to the tension in the room. "Hmmm," he began, "if Mr. Moore made this offer to you, would you accept it?"

"Yes, I would," Rick said. "Certainly, I would. It's a good deal," he insisted, completely unaware of our intention.

"OK, then sign here," Michel said, making a dramatic show of flipping the contract around and pushing it across the table.

Rick's jaw dropped. He didn't see this coming. He allowed a long silence. "Well, I'll...I'll...I'll have to think about it," he stammered awkwardly. "I'll sleep on it and sign tomorrow."

"Wonderful," my masterful lawyer replied. "You have stated in front of everybody here that you're going to sign. You're going to sell based on these terms."

The meeting ended. Rick didn't look at me. And I averted my gaze as well. I had cottoned on to what was happening here. Not long afterward, I learned that Rick had already hired a VP from North American Van Lines to take my place as operator of MJ Campbell, the success of which I had made happen. All this contributed to my realization that I did want to fight for the company.

After some tense negotiations the following day, Rick relented and agreed to sell.

I would be the sole owner and president of an expanding moving enterprise. It was the scariest moment of my life.

I had assigned myself my own weakness: dealing with financial matters. And the biggest challenge was right in front of me. I had to come up with $400,000!

Bernardine and I talked it through. God bless her, she was willing to take the risk with me. And to make the sacrifices. You can't claim to be an entrepreneur if you can't make sacrifices. We certainly did.

I sold nearly everything, including our beautiful house in the popular Montréal suburb of Beaconsfield. The house, with a large garden, was in an exclusive area on the lakefront. We were living high off the hog, having done well with selling TC Moore. We loved that house. By this point, Bernardine had given birth to Matthew, the eldest of our two sons. It was a great place to raise children. But it had to go.

We moved from a spacious 5,500-square-foot house to a rented semi-detached 1,400-square-foot townhouse in Mississauga. Most of our furniture had to be stored. It was stressful to go back to basics, feeling broke and watching every penny. Bernardine didn't know Toronto and had to settle into a new community as a young mother.

Then, more challenge arose. As I was pulling together the money, another financial problem emerged that Rick had neglected to tell me about. MJ Campbell was nearly insolvent. The line of credit was maxed out. We had been taking too much money out of the business. I went to the Bank of Montreal, the company lender. I sat across from the BMO manager as I made my case. I'll never forget his words to me: "Tim, I think you should go look for another bank."

It's hard to convey how alarming that was to hear, especially when I was buying the company. Unfortunately, the truth about banks is that if one doesn't want you, it's unlikely any of the others will either.

I was terrified. But I did my best to exude confidence. I had learned how to do that.

One or two other banks dismissed us. Our balance sheet was not strong enough. No one would take us on as a client. I kept a conversation going—my sales pitch, really—with the Bank of Montreal. They didn't know me—or my work ethic. They had only had a relationship with Rick. I encouraged them to stick with us and watch our bottom line, pressing my case about how we were driven to succeed. I introduced the manager to our employees, to prove my point about the quality of our people. I notified the manager about every new contract we won. I was actively building a relationship with them, a bit like wooing a suspicious, reluctant date!

Within a year, I had $250,000 cash in the bank. The Bank of Montreal loved us. I had proven myself. Their initial refusal to back me was seared into my brain. Ultimately, it felt good to know that my belief in myself had been vindicated.

I was in the driver's seat, and I had a vision for where I wanted to go.

Chapter 4

Be Different or Die

To do what everybody else has done for thirty years is not a challenge. To innovate, create, and redesign for tomorrow is my idea of what business is all about.

LOU PRITCHETT
Vice-President Sales, Procter & Gamble

I WAS IN ENTREPRENEURIAL OVERDRIVE, RESEARCHING THE moving sector to figure out how to compete effectively. In the late 1970s and early 1980s, the moving business in Canada was dominated by a half-dozen or so large companies, such as Kenwood, Mayflower Transit, Sentinel, Western Moving & Storage, and A&F Baillargeon Express Inc., many of which had been in business since the 1930s and 1940s.

My fear propelled me to hustle and innovate and lead like never before. Entrepreneurs often live in the extreme. Recently, Gordon Lownds, the co-founder and CEO of Sleep Country Canada, wrote a candid memoir, *Cracking Up*, in which he describes his addiction to cocaine during a crazy period of his life. Throughout the three-year addiction, he estimates he spent over $700,000 on the drug. As a high-functioning addict, he says, his ability to drive the mattress business wasn't impaired. While on his recovery journey, spurred on by hitting "rock bottom" via an overdose and an arrest, he was still able to create the successful hearing aid retailer ListenUP! Canada.

I never did anything that extreme. I worked hard. That was my addiction. Bernardine helped by creating a calm home environment. She'd always ground me, welcoming me home from the wars of my business life. Often, she would sit me down and treat me to a "home spa" treatment, giving me a manicure and pedicure, trimming my eyebrows. To this day, she likes to lay out my clothes to wear. It is her way of making my life easier.

The decision to take on ownership of the company marked the beginning of my fiscal education. I implemented daily assessments of our financial statements and our bank position. I didn't want any surprises. I had had enough of those! Every month, within a week and a half, I would examine where we were in profit and loss. It was very important to me that I got financial statements on a timely basis. The other consistent guideline for me was, what's my bank position today? Is the line of credit up or down? I was relentless. I would compare our sales for each quarter to the year before. When you know what's going on, you can react to the situation calmly. I knew, for example, that the first four months of the year were not good. Few people did moves in the dead of winter. I was able to plan for that. I was taking the pulse of the business, monitoring its health like a good doctor would monitor a patient.

Within seven or eight months, I'd paid down the credit line and had roughly $250,000 in the bank—to my great relief! My patient was going to live!

Right out of the gate, I had made a sneaky little marketing move. I put the *A* in the company name, making it AMJ Campbell, so that it would be top of the list in the *Yellow Pages*. Everybody advertised in the *Yellow*

Pages. There were over three hundred moving companies listed, taking up over twenty pages. And these were listed alphabetically. Why would I want my company listed halfway down in the *M* section? Soon many companies followed my little trick.

I also made my first significant decision as majority owner: AMJ Campbell had to push farther into Western Canada. I was watching Canada's economic news. A vibrant oil industry in Alberta meant that many resource companies were moving employees to Calgary, Edmonton, Fort McMurray, and other booming oil towns. I knew we had to grab more of that ballooning business.

Rick and I had secured a toehold in the West by purchasing a small, money-losing and underperforming Edmonton company called Hooper's Moving & Storage. The $20,000 deal gave us a few aging trucks, moving equipment, and some office furniture. It was a point of entry for Western expansion—*if* we could turn Hooper's around. The question was: Who should run it for AMJ Campbell?

My brother, Terry, who'd helped me with some moves in Montréal during the mid-1970s, had since moved to Vancouver and was working as the western sales manager for the electronics giant Philips, responsible for all sales from Thunder Bay to Vancouver. We'd had a few discussions about him joining me in the moving business if a good opportunity arose. This was the moment. Knowing his contacts in Western Canada would be very valuable, I called him and made my pitch, which included the option for him to buy a 10 percent stake in our western operations.

He promptly borrowed $7,000 from our mother and bought into the company. A month later, he and his wife, Lynne, and their young daughter were living in Edmonton. Although Terry knew little about the moving industry, he quickly learned the ropes. He had moved to

Alberta in June, the busiest time of year for a moving company as that's when many leases expire. Terry drove the trucks himself to ensure all the jobs were completed. A year later, Terry and Lynne relocated to Calgary when we realized that it was a busier market than Edmonton.

Over the next five years, Terry and his team grew our Calgary business at an astonishing rate, eventually turning it into the biggest mover in the city. Terry secured important clients like Canadian Airlines and Petro-Canada. AMJ Campbell completed moves for thousands of their employees. Calgary soon became AMJ Campbell's second-largest operation outside of Toronto with a 100,000-square-foot warehouse facility—larger than a football field.

Terry had started off in Calgary with four walls and a small building. In addition to his Edmonton and Calgary offices, he started satellite operations in Red Deer, Fort McMurray, Medicine Hat, and Winnipeg. In 1995, he won the moving industry's award of excellence, competing against 250 other major movers in Canada. By 1998, they had three hundred trucks and trailers and executed over three thousand moves a year, pulling in nearly $19 million in annual revenue.

Terry liked the business. "It was exciting to build a company from such a small beginning," he recalls. "It was exciting to see our sales figures increase each month. Every day is different in the moving industry. You didn't know what you'd see each day."

He was also brilliant at marketing. He partnered with sports teams who often had to move newly acquired players and their families to the home city. Terry struck deals with the Calgary Flames of the NHL and the Calgary Stampeders, the local CFL team. AMJ Campbell offered a significant discount on moving costs in exchange for being named the "Official Mover" for the teams in their advertising. The exposure it earned us was invaluable.

I negotiated a similar deal with Canada's Olympic team, making AMJ Campbell "Canada's Olympic Mover" responsible for transporting all athlete equipment, including to training events before the Games. For the 1994 Winter Games in Lillehammer, Norway, for example, we transported containers by ship and air, the contents of which included skis, skates, luges, wine, beer, maple syrup, peanut butter, Halls cough drops, and thirty cartons of bathrobes.

Our tag line was: "AMJ CAMPBELL VAN LINES—MOVING OUR ATHLETES TO THEIR OLYMPIC DREAMS." We also capitalized on our relationship with the Olympics to sponsor key athletes and offered them free leased cars.

It was Terry, though, who perfected these "contra" deals. Such arrangements grew to include deals with the Toronto Maple Leafs, Toronto Raptors, Montreal Canadiens, Ottawa Senators, BC Lions, and more. Essentially, we became the official mover of pro sports clubs, handling moves for all athletes connected to those teams. The result was publicity we could never have afforded to pay for normally.

An added marketing bonus was that many of those athletes, such as NHLer Lanny McDonald, attended our corporate functions and receptions. Our clients were always thrilled to meet these star players, a fact that often secured the next year's business.

Terry also implemented the "Move of the Game" promotion. Highly branded with our name, a draw was made at the beginning of a game to give two fans seated in the nosebleed section a move to front-row seats. It was very popular.

Similarly, Terry traded moving services for ad time with local media companies. Terry wanted everyone in Calgary to recognize the AMJ Campbell brand. His efforts using sports and media promotions made it happen. Another clever idea was to put our logo and phone number on the top of our trucks so that the information was visible to people working above in office buildings.

Terry and I were constantly on the hunt for an edge over our competitors, always developing innovative ideas for enticing potential customers. At various times we offered different promotions: a Move and Fly program with Canadian Airlines whereby customers earned a frequent-flyer point for every dollar they spent on moving; coupons for dinners at restaurants such as Swiss Chalet (as we owned two franchises); mortgage rate rebates of 0.25 percent with TD Bank; discounts at Hertz and at Westin Hotels; hardware store gift certificates; home cleaning services; and move-in gift packs with cleaning supplies for the customer's new house.

These ideas also earned us media attention. A *Financial Post* article from 1993 described our offerings as "perks by the truckload." In all those cases, our customers received something extra, and we gained credibility by partnering with established brands and businesses.

We realized that marketing had to involve thinking outside the (moving) box.

After the expansion in the West, it was a blur of deals, funded by loans and internal cash flow, to reach into all corners of the country. My belief has always been that when you buy a company, you transition the name over time. Don't retain the old brand. During the 1980s, each company we acquired was quickly taken under the recognizable AMJ Campbell banner. This approach was contrasted by A&F Baillargeon Express, a huge competitor of ours that often retained an acquired company's name. The result was a patchwork of companies with no unifying branding—a fact that I think contributed to their bankruptcy.

Our second early acquisition was in Ottawa, where we paid $200,000 for moving equipment and a licence. Despite the large price tag, it was very good value. Their municipal and provincial licences were gold. Plus, government business was plentiful and lucrative at the time, growing to comprise roughly 20 percent of our sales.

In 1983, we pushed into New Brunswick by purchasing Tuck's in Moncton and moving into Fredericton. The next year we added St. Catharines and London in Southern Ontario. In 1985, we expanded into Halifax and Winnipeg.

Another pivotal moment came in 1984, when I made the highly risky but ultimately correct and lucrative decision to switch our US-based affiliate van line. At that time, any Canadian moving company with expansion ambitions had to be connected to an American van line company. (There were six US-based van lines competing nationally in Canada then: North American Van Lines, United Van Lines, Mayflower Transit, Allied Van Lines, MacCosham Van Lines, and Atlas Van Lines.) AMJ Campbell had been part of North American Van Lines for about twenty-five years, and we paid them 10 percent of revenues for the honour of being affiliated with them. The relationship was like being a franchisee. As a North American "agent," we were connected but separate and benefitted from centralized dispatch, billing, and claim settlements. In practical terms, it meant that anyone calling North American Van Lines about a move within Canada was supposed to be directed to us, as an affiliate mover.

Except that didn't always happen. In fact, North American had their own agents in Canada that competed with us directly for business.

Basically, North American was pitting their agents against ours! They were the only one to do that. I believed the conflict of interest was unconscionable—something I spoke to the media about. Even with that conflict, AMJ Campbell represented 28 percent of North American's national corporate business in Canada. Despite all the resulting revenue we sent them, they treated us like an annoying younger brother.

Then, when we opened an office in Fort McMurray, North American's president of Canadian operations, Dick Shirk, threatened to sue us if we didn't immediately close the business. (And he did so in an impersonal letter, when he should have called me directly to find a resolution.) "They refused to allow us to expand," I told the *Toronto Star* in early 1985.

The tension between our company and North American increased further after I successfully poached Jackie Stewart, that company's top salesperson, from their Toronto subsidiary, causing their annual sales to instantly drop by $2 million. North American countered by threatening to cancel our agent status. The relationship was obviously broken and, in my opinion, beyond fixing.

When our contract with North American expired in December 1984, I cut them loose and switched to Indiana-based Atlas Van Lines, the smallest van line in Canada. The move was a tremendous gamble, mainly because Atlas was tiny compared to North American (then owned by PepsiCo). We risked losing millions of dollars in revenue if Atlas couldn't push business our way. But Atlas's chief financial officer (and later president) Doug Auld was smart and made me an irresistible offer that mitigated some of that risk: Atlas would repaint all our trucks (a value of roughly $350,000), provide a year's worth of free advertising literature, and give us a $1 million signing bonus—an unheard of sum in the industry, and one that prompted a lot of celebrating at our head office. Mayflower Transit, a large Atlas competitor, also offered us a $1 million signing bonus, but the Atlas deal—signed on my fortieth birthday (December 7, 1984)—was much sweeter. For its part, Atlas would get 5–10 percent of the fees levied on moves greater than 240 kilometres. Doug Auld and I also negotiated a volume rebate and bonus programs that rewarded us for increasing our sales volumes—an incentive system that benefitted both sides, but which had proven impossible to wrangle from North American. If North American had been smart, we would have stayed with them. AMJ Campbell was loyal by nature. Soon after, 8 AMJ Campbell agents were in the top 10 of Atlas's 140 agents in North America.

But all that success and expansion heightened the stress of running the business. I could never escape it—even when on an airplane. One time, I was relaxing on a flight while having a drink. A flight attendant distributed copies of a newspaper. I took one and opened it. There was a story about AMJ Campbell movers who had loaded up a van after emptying the contents of a condo. They were about to close the rear door of the truck when the owner showed up and threatened to call the police. "What do you think you're doing with my stuff?" he shouted. The superintendent of the building had mistakenly given the movers the wrong condo key.

During all this expansion, a central reason for our success was our relationships with people. I genuinely enjoy talking to others about life and business. We're social animals. My ability to develop contacts was my strong suit. I often feel that my personality and enjoyment of people were strong elements of our success. Customers, particularly potential ones, need to feel a level of trust in you.

How was I different? I like to believe that, in part, it was the emphasis I put on politeness. I didn't tolerate rude behaviour—not in my employees and not in my customers—which may come as a surprise to some people. Shouldn't you always do business, even if your client is a jerk? No. I'm a little bit of a rebel on some matters. If I see something that's not right, I take a stance. Back in the days of TC Moore Transport, I once refused to execute a move after the client was disrespectful to my receptionist—who happened to be Bernardine at the time. His was the second move of the day, and I was running a bit late. He called up Bernardine and hollered at her, "Tell Tim to get his ass over here!" She tried to appease him, saying I would be there shortly. In fact, one of my moving trucks was en route to his place. But then twenty minutes later, he called Bernardine again, shouting like a madman. Bernardine called me, and I told her to take a bus—we only had one car—to go to the customer's house and tell the movers who were about to arrive to turn back. She did. The customer was incensed. But manners matter—sometimes more than money. In my experience, 95 percent of people are great. Only 5 percent are not; you don't want to do business with them.

As part of my early hustling strategy, I would make lists of the large companies that moved a lot of employees. I would identify who the players were, who made the decisions. I made cold calls to the secretaries of the executives I wanted to get in to see. (Those were the days before voicemail.) I would treat them like gold. Sometimes, if I persisted too much, the secretary might get snappy. But I used my sense of humour. I was polite. If your interest in people is genuine, it's easy to engage in conversation.

This approach landed me TD Bank—eventually. The secretary of the vice-president, Ross Thompson, who made relocation decisions, finally put my call through to her boss.

"Hello, it's Tim Moore," I began. "From AMJ Campbell."

"Yeah, I know who you are," he said curtly. "What do you want?"

It was not a friendly beginning. But this is the kind of response you will often get on a cold call. I ignored his gruff response and explained that we had a great product, that we were unique, that we were coast to coast. All I wanted was a few minutes of his time in person to make my presentation.

He agreed to see me. His office was in the TD Tower in Toronto. I dressed in a smart Harry Rosen suit, along with suspenders, a flashy tie, and cowboy boots. Burgundy snakeskin cowboy boots. They were comfortable. What can I say? The bonus was that my attire got me noticed. I was memorable!

Generally, an executive will give you five minutes to make your pitch. But when you get face to face, the dynamic changes. Politeness comes into play. Personality. Curiosity. Charm. All the things that are hard to convey over a phone. I could extend the meeting to an hour. I would ask about their life. Are they married? Do they have children? That sort of thing. Friendly. Without being annoying. In making my pitch about AMJ Campbell, I was always hugely enthusiastic about how we did business. I had always instructed my salespeople never to knock the competition. It's a low-class way to conduct business, in my opinion. I talked about the talent and quality of the people in our company. I emphasized our level of professionalism and service. You must believe in what you do. You must be happy, upbeat, compelling. When you're enthusiastic, it's contagious. There's a big difference between being a good salesperson and being a smart business person. Those are two separate skill sets. I learned how to adjust my approach based on the circumstances.

I also made a judgment about what they were likely paying for moving services. I did my research. I knew what the going rates were. I would come in a little lower and urge them to give us a chance. They often did. And when they didn't, I would often persist in a nice way, and then move on if the answer was still no.

In early 1983, Kraft went out to tender for corporate moving services. We offered to do all the company's moving for $500,000 but we were beaten out on price. I expressed my disappointment, asked in a professional manner for an explanation, said I understood their decision, and wished them luck. Six months later, I got a call from Kraft head office. They regretted choosing the discount mover and had heard of our reputation for service. We were offered all their business.

I understood that you should not burn bridges with clients, even if you don't get the business. I witnessed first-hand how some moving companies handled the disappointment of losing a lucrative contract. Bob Ough, the senior operations manager at Canadian Helicopters, called me up one day to say that we'd won his company's moving contract. He asked me to meet him at the company's Dorval hangar to discuss the details.

At the hangar, as I was approaching his office, I could hear him having a heated, confrontational phone call. I stayed outside the office until I finally heard Bob slam the receiver down. He then welcomed me in and explained that he'd been talking to one of my competitors, the company that had just lost the contract after three years of lacklustre service. Senior management at that moving company, feeling entitled to Bob's business, blew up at him after being told they'd lost the contract. Their response, Bob told me, would guarantee they'd never get another dollar of business from Canadian Helicopters.

Sometimes you win, sometimes you lose, but you have to always be a good sport, even in defeat. AMJ Campbell's deep focus on professionalism and quality service was clearly reflected in the roster of corporate clients that trusted us with relocating their employees to different parts of Canada. Among those clients were: The Bay, Xerox, Simpson's, CIL, Gulf, Mobil, Sun Life, and most of the big banks. No company did more bulk moves than AMJ Campbell.

Some businesses, however, seemed impossible to gain. One was Northern Telecom. We tried very hard to get their business. They would occasionally throw us the odd move to manage. But there was one small moving company in Montréal that got the majority of their contracts.

One of my salesmen, Kevin Devereux, came to me one day with a suspicion that the manager in charge of Northern Telecom moves was on the take. It just didn't make sense that one small moving company was getting all the work.

"Go and have dinner and feel out the situation," I suggested to Kevin.

He did. A few days later, I was in my office when Kevin called me.

"Are you sitting down?" he asked.

I was.

Then he told me "the situation."

What did the Northern Telecom executive want? A kickback of 8 percent cash on all moves.

That was one of the most difficult decisions of my career. I was always generous to corporate customers: paying for dinners, hotel rooms, letting them stay at my cottage. Those are often the costs of doing business. But pay a kickback?

We did for a year and a half. Was it morally correct? No. I was uncomfortable about it. But the business world is not always kind—or moral. You roll with it, sometimes. I'm no angel. As it turned out, the executive lost his job. The moving contract, worth several million dollars in revenue, went out on tender again, and we landed it fair and square.

There are always compromises you must make in business; some you don't like. Another example was my involvement with the Teamsters union. As I noted earlier, I inherited the union when I bought MJ Campbell. I was tough with them. "If you keep pressuring us to get every employee unionized, I will close down the company," I warned them. For six months, we fought. Eventually, I signed the Teamsters contract by agreeing to take care of two union members at MJ Campbell who'd been with them for twenty-five years. As a result, the union backed off their employee-pressure campaign. We maintained a good relationship. I had compromised.

But that decision worked in my favour a few years later. I spotted workers picketing outside a Canada Post sorting station on Dixie Road in Toronto, near our Mississauga office. Antennae always up in search of an opportunity, I acted. I called the Canada Post station and offered the use of our trucks for delivering and retrieving mail during the strike. At a meeting with Canada Post executives, we made a deal: fifteen of our trucks would be continually on call for the duration of the strike, available any time. Canada Post would pay a daily rate for each truck. Without being a union member, I would not have been able to bid on that business.

Fast forward two months, and we hadn't received a single call for our services. Yet, we were billing Canada Post for roughly $150,000 a month. When the strike was finally resolved, Canada Post had never used our trucks. Our company was paid $300,000. A blow to taxpayers. But a nice addition on our bottom line.

In 1984, we opened a new 75,000-square-foot head office and warehouse facility in Mississauga on four acres near Pearson International Airport. The developer wanted $160,000 an acre, but we bargained it down to $109,000 an acre. We spent roughly $1.7 million to build it. This was more than a real estate deal for me. It was a dream realized. In my opinion, the facility was unlike any other moving company headquarters in North America. There were articles about it in many newspapers. Everything about the place projected quality and professionalism. Outside, the stone exterior had our logo emblazoned at the top. The front had a row of big windows. Our clean, smartly designed trucks were arrayed in perfect alignment in the parking lot. Inside, Ethan Allen, a high-quality furnishing and accessory company, set the tone with large, comfortable sofas and quality tables. It was like the lobby of a luxury hotel. There was also a racquetball court, a gym, and a hot tub for employees. Employees did aerobics classes at lunchtime. The boardroom table sat thirty people. Beautiful art graced the walls. Walk through the heavy wooden door to my presidential suite, and it was like something out of a movie featuring a Wall Street banker. The seating area was a sunken living-room style with a fireplace at one end. My large desk was positioned on a dais. There was a bar, a sound system. It got attention.

Our headquarters were an unapologetic celebration of our corporate energy and drive, shared by all our employees. We produced a slick marketing video of our trucks rolling out of the parking lot. It was like a movie trailer for some blockbuster Hollywood drama. I had developed a culture of success. Every Monday morning, sales guru Jackie Stewart would jokingly enter her department and ask, "What location did Tim open this weekend? Where's the new office this week?"

The message to the outside world was clear: AMJ Campbell operated in a rough industry, but we were not a rough company. We did things differently. There's nothing sexy about the moving business. It's a problem-rich business, in fact, full of challenges. But we made it sexy. We made it a luxury service. We had moved the needle, pardon the pun, for what a transport company could be.

Canadian Business magazine described me in May 1989 as "a flamboyant entrepreneur who sports Italian designer suits and burgundy snakeskin [cowboy] boots and who drives a cherry-red convertible Rolls-Royce Corniche."

Yup, I leveraged the attention. I was a living, breathing advertisement for my company. If there had been social media in those days, we would have been all over it. Attention is lucrative. Attention puts you top of mind. I would drive my red Rolls-Royce Corniche convertible to moving industry conventions and park it right out front. *Keep 'em guessing*, I always thought of my competition. Do the unexpected. Be bold.

The 1980s were chaotic, exciting, fun, transformational, and very productive. In a little over ten years, we'd taken AMJ Campbell from a two-office company with $250,000 in annual sales to a thirty-six-branch, coast-to-coast moving powerhouse with annual sales exceeding $57 million and a fleet of ninety trucks and vans. We'd gone from being a little-known regional mover to the national leader.

Among the many headlines we received over those years, my favourite was: "Ex-seminarian Now Has a Flock of Moving Vans."

Chapter 5

Build a Corporate Cult of Excellence

Outstanding leaders go out of their way to boost the self-esteem of their personnel. If people believe in themselves, it's amazing what they can accomplish.

SAMUEL MOORE WALTON
Co-founder of Walmart

The function of leadership is to produce more leaders, not more followers.

RALPH NADER

No matter how brilliant your mind or strategy, if you're playing a solo game, you'll always lose out to a team.

REID HOFFMAN
Co-founder of LinkedIn

I NEVER SPENT A NICKEL ON RECRUITMENT FIRMS. I NEVER put an ad in newspapers looking for key managers. Not once. Even today, with all the digital platforms available for recruitment, I would be unlikely to use them. My approach was simple. I observed people. And then, if

I liked what I saw, I poached them. I looked for personality. Sincerity. Integrity. Positivity. Consistent temperament.

I once hired an optician, Clint Giffin, after seeing how he treated me when I needed new glasses. He was happy, confident, outspoken, positive, and knowledgeable. When I returned to pick up the glasses he'd helped me select, I made my pitch.

"Clint, I think you're working in the wrong profession," I told him, half joking, half serious.

He balked. "I've been an optician for twenty years," he replied, surprised at my ballsy opinion. (You must be direct!) Clearly, he liked what he did—and he was good at it. This was his chosen profession.

I encouraged him to meet me for lunch so I could tell him more about the opportunity of working with us. After two meetings, he decided to jump over to the AMJ Campbell sales team. He was a terrific fit. From eye care to moving. Who would have thought that transition would work?

Another example is Barry Stanton, an Ottawa boy and outstanding football player whom I worked with back in 1972, in my short-lived house-painting business. In the 1980s, I recruited Barry to work at AMJ Campbell. He was outgoing, friendly, always smiling, and a gentleman. Among Barry's many strong traits were his openness to change. He was always amenable to new ideas and adventures, and relocated several times during his career with AMJ Campbell. Like Clint, Barry was loved by everyone who knew him. He was an outstanding, caring, and genuine employee and partner.

I even once hired a waitress in a bar at the Valhalla Inn in Toronto. She had a terrific personality. I liked the way she treated people. She was consistent. Her temperament was unflappable, even with difficult people. My kind of employee.

I made it a practice to ask potential hires what they wanted from their lives. Sometimes, it was just to be part of a good and dynamic company. And that's fine. Other times, people would express to me their dream of success, and I always listened carefully. Many of us have dreams. But they take hard work to realize. I became good at recognizing the people who had what it takes to be successful.

One such person was Leo Thibodeau. He first came to me when he was eighteen years old. He wanted to meet me because he'd heard about the success of the company. I had that grand CEO office in our AMJ Campbell headquarters. At my desk, I had a beautiful burgundy leather chair.

"Come in," I said to him when he entered my office and looked around at the lavish surroundings. We talked for a while, then he asked if he could sit in my chair. I allowed him to take the seat, and he presided over the room with a small smile on his face. He was young and full of energy. He told me his dream. He was goal-oriented, pragmatic, and ambitious.

"Tim, I want this chair," he confessed to me after we had talked at some length. "I want to run a company."

I had watched him and listened carefully. Stars in his eyes. Fire in his belly. "You can have that chair if you work your ass off," I said.

I hired him, and he did work hard. He was a great employee. He moved up and took on more and more responsibilities. Leo left after I did and started an office moving enterprise. He now owns the largest office moving company in Canada.

Another was Joe Gagnon. I hired him when he was young and assigned him to sales. He was very goal-oriented and focussed on promotion. With diligent work and high sales volumes, he moved up in the company. But in the early 2000s, when I had left AMJ Campbell, the new owners told Joe that he wasn't CEO material. Great in sales, but nothing more. They said he didn't have the aptitude.

Then came the f-you move. Joe left. He bought a small moving company—Westmount Moving and Storage—in Montréal. Brought in a key partner. And he quickly turned that little company into a multi-million-dollar operation. I knew Joe had the ability. He was a winner.

Hone your instinct about people—and then trust it. Give them a chance to prove themselves. Don't make judgments about their ability until you've given them a chance to display it.

A huge boost in momentum for our growth at AMJ Campbell came with the hiring of Jackie Stewart, a pioneering figure within the moving industry who put us on the map overnight and became a legend in the business.

In 1980, Jackie was working for the Toronto subsidiary of North American Van Lines and was the company's top salesperson. That feat is doubly impressive when you consider this was a woman working in a male-dominated, sexist industry. (North American Van Lines management interviewed Jackie nine times before finally hiring her, because they were so conflicted about hiring a woman for a sales job.) Despite their hesitation, they obviously made the right choice: Jackie was a sales powerhouse, using her keen attention to detail and strong client relationships to land and, most importantly, maintain big clients. For seven straight years she was the top sales performer in the history of North American Van Lines.

I knew we needed Jackie. Fortunately for me, North American didn't fully appreciate what they had in her, in large part because she was a woman. As Jackie essentially put it: North American's managers were stuck in the previous century. When I met her at a convention in Florida, I made my pitch: she'd immediately be a vice-president at AMJ Campbell, with a seat on the board of directors, and an option to purchase equity in the company, making her a minority owner.

Jackie agreed to join us in May 1981 as director of national sales, though as she jokingly said later, "If I'd known how much money AMJ *didn't* have, I never would have switched." (Evidently my pitch made our circumstances sound rosier than they were.) Nevertheless, Jackie's arrival immediately bolstered our bottom line.

Nearly all her clients followed her from North American, meaning we gained $2 million in annual sales overnight—at the expense of a competitor. North American was not pleased. Jackie's treatment of clients aligned perfectly with our commitment to professional service. When approaching a potential client, she would pledge to personally oversee all the client's moves and be involved in the process right down to selecting the drivers and crew, and she'd be readily available to support the client in any way needed—including on the ground during moves. She was the personification of our tag line, "You deal with us here and at the other end." And because Jackie delivered on that pledge of service from origin to point of destination, her clients remained extremely loyal. And these were large corporate clients, such as the big banks, Canadian Airlines, the Domtar paper company, GM, Imperial Oil, and many more.

Jackie would bring clients to our head office for lunch so they could see for themselves how items were packed, loaded, and handled; she knew the names of her clients' children; she handed out gifts at

Christmas, Easter, and Valentine's. The result of that commitment was measurable: Jackie's annual sales at AMJ Campbell eventually hit $4 million, an industry record at that time in Canada. Her connection with TD Bank alone was worth $1 million a year. "I loved the excitement of growing the company and travelling across the country. We were young, we had fun, and we worked hard," she recalls. "If I was smart, I would have tried to buy half the company!" Asked to summarize the reason for AMJ Campbell's success, she answered with two words: "The friendships." "My clients were my friends. I was part of their lives, and they were part of mine," she added. "I have been exceedingly lucky in my life. I seem to go from one good thing to another, each better than the last. And it's all because of relationships."

The power of Jackie's name in the organization was made plain one day when this story made its way back to our Mississauga head office: Her in-laws, who lived in Victoria, BC, had been waiting in line for a ferry. Near them in the lineup was an AMJ Campbell van.

Her father-in-law walked up to the truck and casually asked the driver, half joking: "Do you know Jackie Stewart?"

"Of course, she's our million-dollar baby!" the driver replied.

Despite being the company's sales workhorse, Jackie wouldn't hesitate to help unpack a shipment if we were short-staffed. And she wasn't alone; at peak times in summer, up to a third of our office workers would be out in the field helping pack boxes. One day, Jackie was helping unpack boxes from a Department of National Defence family move. The defence department was a major client and always expected military-like precision: moves completed on schedule and without mistakes. The federal government also applied hefty penalties for any shortcomings, no matter how small or seemingly ridiculous. For example, there was a $2,000 fine for not wrapping hardcover books individually, and a

$5,000 penalty if your company failed to individually wrap a cane or a sword. You'd get dinged $4,600 for not rolling all rugs separately. It was bureaucratic nonsense that could quickly turn a job into a money-loser for any company. The husband of the military family, a member of the forces, was evidently impressed with Jackie's skill. As she was unpacking a box of glassware, he told her: "I think you could be doing more for the company than unpacking boxes. You should move up or do something else—get a better job." She accepted the comment with a smile, not letting on that she was a senior vice-president who brought in millions of dollars in sales each year.

Jackie and I remain close, even half a century after she made the leap to AMJ Campbell.

"Success is a toss of the dice," she told me. "You don't know where you'll end up, but you've got to take a chance." Jackie took a chance on our small company, and it paid huge dividends to her and us. Every successful business must have at least one superstar salesperson like Jackie.

By the end of the 1980s, with all the rapid expansion of AMJ Campbell we had about one thousand employees across the country. I personally hired hundreds of them, including 95 percent of the key people. By the 1990s, our employees numbered close to three thousand.

The key is to have the right people at the top. Leadership style filters down. Consider what's happening with the Trump administration. If lying and immorality are normalized, then everyone feels they have permission to follow suit. Running a country is like running a company. People follow you and the way in which you conduct yourself.

I set standards for how I expected my employees to behave:

- Motivate people through kindness, generosity, and a sense of humour.
- Send thank-you notes or make a point of saying thank you for a job well done.
- Don't ever yell or severely criticize one employee over another.
- Don't allow a show of disrespect toward a customer or another employee.
- Have zero tolerance for sexual harassment.
- Encourage employees to address a complaint about another employee directly rather than through office gossip.
- Treat all employees equally, with no obvious favouritism.

You need people with the right attitude, the right work ethic. Having that shared value system also made decisions easier. I always consulted the opinions of my colleagues. I wasn't surrounded by yes men or yes women. I don't know everything. Not by a long shot. I listened to their points of view. And I trusted their input.

Another strategy to building a solid company was to always encourage key employees to buy shares. That way, they're tied to the company. They have a vested interest in staying for the long term and working hard to make the company profitable. It creates loyalty. When you're running a national company involving many satellite operations, you absolutely need to have committed managers to ensure each one runs productively and profitably.

That approach worked well with my brother Terry, who bought 10 percent of the Calgary operation, and with my brother, Ted, and his partners, Craig Miller and Barry Stanton, who all bought shares in our Ottawa group.

My cousin, Neil West, left his job managing a drugstore in Montréal to have a sales role in the Toronto operation and eventually became an equity partner in the St. Catharines business. Today, he works in the Halifax operation.

Canadian Business magazine once described my strategy as "enlightened nepotism." And it worked: the business grew rapidly after Ted and Terry joined in the late 1970s. That's because any value surrendered by selling to an employee is easily recovered through the growth of the business under their leadership. You maintain majority control, while adding a committed partner. There's only an upside.

It's better to have a smaller piece of a growing pie than a larger piece of a stagnant one. I always undervalued my companies when selling equity to employees in order to make it easier for them to join as partners. Any value lost through discounting was always returned tenfold, thanks to their contributions.

I had a similar approach to partnerships with outside investors. In fact, partnerships became a signature feature of how I was able to grow many of my businesses. Again, the key is to retain controlling interest so you can have a strong voice on major decisions. In my career, I have had about 175 partners. That's a huge number. But it was the only way to grow those enterprises. You can't be everywhere. I wouldn't expand to a new office until I had a good partner. And as I have said, it all comes down to identifying the right people. I applied the same principle I had for hiring people as I did for finding business partners. You will hear me say this again and again: Look for integrity, determination, a pleasant personality, drive.

Out of all those partnerships, I experienced problems only three or four times. One was with a prominent personality in Ottawa. I had met him several times and liked him very much. We always had great exchanges. Some of my friends warned me against him, saying not to trust him, but I always like to make up my own mind. He was keen to do business with me, and I figured he would be a good partner because of his connections. So, I got him involved as an investor in two of my businesses.

All was well for several years. No problems. We were always cordial. But one day, we met for lunch. Bernardine had come along because our meetings were often more social than business-oriented. Out of nowhere, he announced that he wanted out of one of the ventures we had together. He was experiencing health issues and with advancing age, he wanted to get his money out. I was surprised—he had given me no warning. I explained that I understood his reasons. But the timing wasn't right, I said. He would only get 7 percent return on his investment if he divested now.

He suddenly exploded in anger. "I don't get into business to only get 7 percent on my investment," he boomed. I had never seen this side of him. He carried on without restraint in a public setting.

Bernardine promptly got up from the table. She wasn't going to listen to this tirade.

In the end, I bought him out of that particular venture, as he insisted, delivering 7 percent on his investment. In the other business of mine in which he was a partner, he remained invested, which was a good decision on his part. In approximately ten years, he received $800,000 on a $250,000 outlay.

This soured partnership was an anomaly, though. Over 95 percent of the partners I had in various businesses were excellent financial collaborators. They all made good money from their investments with my businesses.

This philosophy to secure commitment from others in growing my businesses extended to making employees feel accountable throughout the ranks. We were among the first moving companies to put our drivers and packers on contract, which in practice made each employee an entrepreneur in their own right. They got a percentage of everything they did, and they paid their own gas, labour, and up to $250 in claims. They had a moral and financial obligation. It would come out of *their* pockets if they didn't do well.

I had no patience for unprofessionalism. You work harder on contract, but you make more. Not surprisingly, service improved and the number of claims for damaged goods dropped noticeably after we said that drivers had to pay the first $200 of every claim. They were motivated to be cautious and careful. And fewer claims meant less bureaucratic work for managers at our head office.

It was a novel approach, and it achieved the desired two-pronged result: Our reputation for service was impeccable, and some of our movers were making $65,000 a year. Our truck owners, although having to pay for expenses like gas, labour, and licensing, were all earning more than $100,000 annually. And this was during the 1980s!

Plus, there was profit-sharing for all the branch managers, whereby they got 10 percent of pre-tax profits. In all cases, it gave them a sense of ownership, which made them feel instantly accountable for their own performance. Similarly, packing and moving staff could earn a seventy-five-dollar bonus per move, based on the results of three customer surveys.

I strongly believed that the best way to run a company was to spread the wealth—and the responsibility—around. The results are evident in a letter we received following a successful move we completed for the City of Mississauga, which had relocated to a new City Hall. "It was a very smoothly executed effort," wrote City Manager D. A. Lychak. "Everyone involved—from the people who estimated your tender costs to the strategic planning and coordination of the move, to the actual loading and unloading process—deserve[s] a sincere thank you for a job very well and professionally done."

What more could you want from a customer?

Our approach to excellent service was the same across all branches. At his Calgary office, Terry received the following letter from customer Doug Bell:

> *Dear Mr. Moore:*
>
> *I received an AMJ customer feedback form in the mail last week and I wanted to share some of my thoughts with you.... Reading the form also brought the realization that I was reading the last chapter in a story that began approximately seven years ago with our move to St. John's, Newfoundland. My first introduction to AMJ was a visit from Konny Shaw to size up and plan the move. At the time, I thought I would be back in Calgary in 12–18 months. I remember being very impressed by her customer focus—little did I know how good the customer focus was in AMJ. AMJ has played a significant role in my world in the years since this first visit with moves from:*
>
> - *Calgary to Paradise, NF and Calgary goods to storage*
> - *Susan's move from Newfoundland to Victoria*
> - *My mother's move from Calgary to Victoria*
> - *My move from Paradise to a house in St. John's*
> - *St. John's to Calgary and then to Chemainus*
> - *Calgary goods in storage to Chemainus*

Excellent customer service with clear attention to detail has been a common theme throughout all of these moves. I have always felt that I have been in good hands while your organization planned and executed these moves. Thanks are due to many of your employees. Recognizing the risk in leaving someone out, and I am sure I am, a critical few stand out in my mind. Konny Shaw and Doug Buchan from Calgary and Paul Budden in Newfoundland have all played a major role in achieving the outstanding level of customer service in my moves.

Good moves, good memories of these moves.

Over the years, our customers came to expect such service. And we delivered. Interpersonal skills and personality are vital in the service industry. They are traits that help guarantee satisfied customers and help generate word-of-mouth referrals, which was the source of 75 percent of our business. It's like Jeff Bezos once said, "A brand for a company is like a reputation for a person. You earn reputation by trying to do hard things well." That's what we did at AMJ Campbell.

AMJ Campbell was a family not just figuratively but literally. I brought my mother in to work in the accounting department. Everyone, even our senior staff, called her "Mom." Bernardine was an important asset as well. Everybody met her at conventions. She was an example to the staff. If you had a problem with Bernardine, you had to look at yourself. She was always gracious, friendly, and caring. She made me look good. The right partner can do that. Think of how the partners of political leaders reflect good (and sometimes not so good) attributes of the other. Melania Trump, whom I do not admire, somehow softens Donald

Trump, redeems him in a way, which is why people say that she has power over him. He needs her! Michelle Obama was the fun to Barack's seriousness. Another example is President Emmanuel Macron and his wife, Brigitte, who is almost twenty-five years his senior and was once his teacher. That shove she gave him, which was caught on video as they were disembarking a plane in May 2025, displayed what many have said privately about that relationship—that she infantilizes him.

Having a good partnership at home is critical to success. I always encouraged families to come into the business, and then I would encourage them to bring in more family members. Wives and husbands and brothers and sisters and uncles and nieces and nephews. Twelve different families were involved with the company in the early stages, with most of them owning shares. By 1989, it was up to seventeen families. Eventually, we had forty-six families involved. Families share values. They want to support one another. And they trust each other. It was a winning strategy. The danger, of course, was if the relationships didn't work out. That happens in families. The dynamics can be fraught. But in my experience the benefits outweighed any disadvantages.

No one in the country had family ties and stock ownership like we did. We were a cult, a different breed, close-knit. We drew up family trees to show all the interconnections between our employees. Everyone was deeply proud of what we created.

I don't think anyone has better captured the feeling of being an AMJ Campbell employee than Carol Davis, a long-time friend and former company vice-president:

> *Working for AMJ Campbell was a bit like being a member of a very large, extended family. The dynamics are similar. There are deep emotional bonds, shared experiences and memories, ongoing sibling*

> *rivalries, and ties that are virtually impossible to sever. Being part of the group was like being invited into some kind of charmed circle. It served to reinforce your own self-esteem and sense of being special. It didn't matter what your actual job was—salesperson, customer-service representative, dispatcher, driver, packer, accounting clerk, or general manager—the atmosphere around the company had so much esprit de corps and was so nurturing that you began to believe that your efforts were appreciated and what you did made a difference. Even if you hadn't always been a high achiever, you became one. There was something about being in the company of so many exceptional people that made an individual want to strive to reach their personal best, if for no other reason than to prove to yourself that you truly deserved to be part of the group. Basking in the glow of the approval you received made you want to do more, work harder, and become even better.*

As a result of our cult-like cohesion as a company we didn't lose a single employee to the competition during the 1980s. Fifteen years later, five of my original drivers were still with the company, a testament to employee-friendly culture I'd nurtured from the beginning. I encouraged employees to take courses for self-improvement. The Dale Carnegie approach to leadership and public speaking had helped me, and I know others who've benefitted greatly from programs like Toastmasters. It's important to encourage your employees to grow and improve their skills. They will gain obvious personal dividends, and so will your company because the employees' expanded self-confidence will aid everything from sales to referrals. Many people don't want to improve. And that's okay. But for those who do, don't underestimate how far they can go. If they have the drive, improvement will follow.

We were not just movers of furniture. We were moving our employees to new possibilities, to new wealth, to new confidence. I wanted to help people in their lives, to earn good money. In many cases, I helped people become millionaires, something I'm very proud of. There was no way any of our employees could go to a better moving company. We had the best brand of service. Our product was unbeatable. The explosive expansion and success in the 1980s were remarkable in what is, generally, a low-margin, high–labour-cost business.

What was driving me? Well, I wanted to make money. I love making money. But that's not all. That, by itself, is just a transactional thing. I have a joy for life. Period. If I could, I would want to be young forever. I believe that if we're all going to work hard, we must have a hell of a good time doing it. In addition to offering share options in the company, internal awards, and generous benefit programs, fun was also my strategy for attracting and retaining employees. It was a work-hard-play-hard philosophy.

The reason I observed (and soon hired) the waitress at the Valhalla Inn in Toronto is that every Thursday evening, after work, we all went to that hotel to have a drink, a bite to eat, and generally have fun. We were in our thirties, full of energy and enthusiasm.

I would encourage people to come to headquarters for coffee and donuts on Saturday mornings. It was like Grand Central Station in our head office! We gathered just to connect, to talk about silly things in our lives, and the serious stuff, too. It was a bonding exercise. Maybe some employees came to have access to me. I had an open-door policy—always—to the drivers, the managers, and the receptionist—the position

I believe is the most important in a company. I forbade my secretary to say, "You can't come in to see Tim." Sure, they might have to make an appointment if I was busy, but I never thought I was too high-and-mighty to speak to anyone. I was interested in them. Empathetic. Sympathetic. I like to think people had a comfort level with me. I felt that if an employee was fearful of me, then maybe they had done something bad. If a mistake had been made, confess it. Come in. Let's discuss it. I would excuse a mistake once, maybe twice. But not a third time. Every day that I was in the office, I walked the floor and through the warehouse to talk to employees, which numbered close to one hundred. I asked about what was going on, what problems they might have encountered.

We had many brainstorming sessions. I wanted everyone to contribute. My assistant, Kim Boydell, described them as "like a category-five tornado of ideas, enthusiasm, and side notes that could lead us anywhere from expanding our moving company into intergalactic shipping (seriously!) to the shocking discovery of Tim having an unexpected affinity for knitting. In his mind, even the most absurd subjects could turn into viable business proposals." I should add that this comment came from a book she wrote called *The Tasmanian Devil Diaries: Inside the Whirlwind World of Tim Moore's Moving Empire*. Spoiler alert: Few of her anecdotes are true! I know nothing about knitting. And I never did enthuse about how moving services could monetize ecological consciousness by repurposing cardboard boxes into eco-friendly furniture.

Nonetheless, there was tremendous energy in the company. Every year, for over a decade, a group of key partners went on a ski trip to Aspen or Vail. We wore identical ski outfits—in red and white—with AMJ Campbell insignia on our jackets. We looked like a professional ski team. We danced on the tables in our ski boots in the raucous après-ski bars. One winter, one of the partners got involved with a woman at Aspen. He was married, and later, when he returned home, he divorced his wife. At a company gathering a few months later, he introduced his new partner—a young, beautiful woman—to Bernardine. She asked politely how they met. When the woman said Aspen, Bernardine's face registered a certain knowing every husband would recognize.

That was the end of my ski trips to Aspen! Bernardine could see only too well the crazy fun we were having. I was not innocent. No choir boy. Kim Boydell once said to me, "What will you pay me NOT to write a book about you?" There were temptations with so much travel. I was not a perfect husband. But I have always been in love with Bernardine. And always will be.

All of us were driven to succeed and make money. One of the partners started using the AMJ initials to stand for Another Magnificent Job. We all pitched in when necessary. No one was considered above doing certain jobs. Humility was important. Quite frankly, I don't know any other way to be. I will never forget going to CTV company headquarters to have a meeting with a top executive. I was waiting in the lobby and the receptionist suggested I go to the kitchen to get a cup of coffee while I waited. I did. A man there offered to pour me a cup, handing it to me. I introduced myself as a corporate mover with AMJ Campbell. He then introduced himself: he was the CEO. And he's serving me coffee? That's an important lesson. You are no better than anyone else.

I would tell my employees, "I'm here to produce and pay my way. If I don't produce with sales or administratively, then I'm gone." Sales managers were told to lead by example. Roughly 70–80 percent of their time should be devoted to business development, I instructed them. No more than 30 percent of their time should be focussed on administrative matters. Sales personnel should be given specific sales targets on a monthly, quarterly, and annual basis. Weekly sales reports were part of their job. I wanted the details to know if we were on track. Salespeople were expected to turn a profit of 8–12 percent. Bonuses were part of the remuneration package for exceeding targets. Sales costs should not exceed 10–11 percent. If sales are $500,000 then the total employee cost to the company should be in the $50,000 range. I had the revenue picture carefully documented with clear expectations.

It was competitive in a healthy way. We had an intercom in our headquarters that held about one hundred employees. When we acquired a major new contract, it would be announced on the loudspeaker. Always, the announcement was that "WE" had landed a new piece of business and the people involved were congratulated.

I didn't believe in having five-year or ten-year plans, as some business programs suggest. If people find them helpful, to each his own. But in my experience, I've seen many entrepreneurs get caught up—and delayed—by spending too much money, energy, and time on producing a business plan. Obviously, some financing plans require a business plan. Generally, for me, if I like an idea, I just go for it—and start. I had goals, but I never wrote them down in a document. I mean, what are goals if not dreams with a deadline? They're important to have. Regularly, I would set goals such as opening a new office or a revenue goal.

To encourage team spirit, we ran silly, fun competitions. Who could wear the craziest tie? The most colourful tie? I once owned a tie that had little people on it. Well, I thought they were just little people. I put it away when someone pointed out to me that the small figures were actually bare-breasted women! Some employees followed my love of wearing cowboy boots. I insisted that employees dress for success.

When someone did a good job, I gave them a gift certificate to Harry Rosen, the venerable menswear store, to buy some nice clothes. We had our shirts monogrammed on the collars. We made a point of wearing fancy cufflinks, comparing with each other if we found unusual ones, like the pair I bought with fish on them. The truck drivers wore uniforms with ties. Swearing was not allowed on the premises or in the trucks.

We were gentleman movers.

The competition extended to hairstyles. I once decided to get an afro by having a permanent curl put in my hair. When I came home, Bernardine took one look at me, screamed, and ran away! She didn't recognize me! The next week, Terry came in with an afro. And the week after that, Ted came in with a wig in the style of an afro. The three Moore brothers were always game for "moore" of anything!

The funny things we did extended to the parties and events we held for corporate clients. Each year, our gala for clients got bigger and bigger to the point that we were entertaining almost four hundred people at a large hotel. There was always a theme. One year, we decided that the senior managers—about fifty of us—should dress up as monks. Down the escalator we came at the Harbour Castle Hotel in Toronto, two at a time, dressed in monks' habits. Another year, we hired a hypnotist, inviting clients up on the stage. Crazy? Maybe. But memorable. Our clients loved us. Of our business, 80 percent came from corporate clients for relocations of their employees both within Canada and internationally. We held Valentine's parties, Hallowe'en parties, Christmas parties, lunch parties, and sailing trips on Lake Ontario in the summers.

Such was my appreciation for the loyalty of our customers and the hard work of our top employees that I would do almost anything—within reason—to show it. One time, I got a call from Allan Coulson, one of our outstanding producers in Western Canada. He told me he was coming to Toronto for three days and asked if he could possibly stay with me at my condo at Palace Pier in the city's west end. This was not a typical request, but I said yes. Allan called again the following day, this time asking if Dean Rennie, a female sales rep, could also stay with me. I figured hosting two guests was no worse than hosting one so, again, I agreed, provided he didn't mind bunking with me in my king-sized bed.

"No problem," he told me.

A day later, Allan mentioned the trip to one of our major client contacts at Canadian Airlines, who asked Allan if he could join, too. Again, Allan called me and again I relented, noting that the guy from Canadian Airlines would have to sleep on my chesterfield. My place was turning into a hotel!

The first night, after getting everyone settled, including Allan next to me in my bed, I was wakened around 11:00 P.M. by Allan's loud snorting. I listened, pretending to be asleep. Eventually, he got up to go into my ensuite bathroom. He closed the door and stayed there for fifteen minutes. Meanwhile, I was lying in bed wondering what the hell I'd agreed to and why Allan was in the bathroom for so long.

When he finally emerged, cigarette smoke poured out of the bathroom. I can't stand the smell of smoke, but too polite to complain, I spent the next few hours struggling to sleep. At 2:30 A.M., Allan started snorting again. He woke up once more, and off he went to the bathroom for another smoke.

I'd had it! I waited half an hour, then decided I might as well get ready for work. After he came out of the bathroom, I went in and found my toothbrush next to Allan's dentures. Yuck! Had he been cleaning them with my toothbrush? I went berserk. I quickly got dressed and drove to work in the early morning darkness.

Later that day, when I saw Allan, I read him the riot act. "No smoking in my condo!" Then I went and bought a new toothbrush!

Another time, a big client in Moncton realized that we were both scheduled for Lasik eye surgery on the same day at the same Toronto clinic. He asked if he could stay with me. Having clearly not learned my lesson, I agreed. We left the clinic together post-procedure. I had one eye bandaged. He had both eyes bandaged. Between the two of us, we had one working eye! We tried to flag down a cab to no avail. We managed to get back to the condo. That night I awoke to find him on all fours, crawling blindly to the bathroom. Getting up to help him, I groggily wondered why I'd—again!—agreed to a sleepover.

But that was my commitment to clients and a reflection of the inclusive culture we developed in the company. An employee at Petro-Canada, a major client, once told me: "A day without giving AMJ Campbell a move is like a day without sunshine." The competition didn't know how we did it. They took shots at us. They couldn't figure out how we came out of nowhere and succeeded so quickly.

But we were unstoppable.

Chapter 6

Take the Bull by the Horns

When everything seems to be going against you, remember that the airplane takes off against the wind, not with it.

HENRY FORD
Founder of Ford Motor Company

In the middle of difficulty lies opportunity.

Attributed to **ALBERT EINSTEIN**

NO BUSINESS GETS A FREE PASS. THERE WILL ALWAYS BE A crisis of one sort or another. For instance, who could have predicted what President Trump would do to create such chaos in the global economy? I have certainly had to handle a few unanticipated crises. After all, stressful challenges arise in every business, in every aspect of life. The key is to deal with them head-on and without delay—don't run away from them. Problems don't disappear. They only magnify. Procrastination is a serious flaw in business and politics today: leaders, entrepreneurs, owners, and managers putting things off, not wanting to deal with complex issues and scary problems. There are many examples. One that stares all of us in the face is the political example of Joe Biden not stepping down from running in the presidential election in 2024. No one wanted to make the decision to push him out because of his declining health, until it was too late. Finally, they did. The world watched as Kamala Harris stepped in to run for president, without much lead time, and lost to Donald Trump. What would have happened if the Democrats had taken decisive action to force Biden to not seek a second term and given another contender a chance to lead the party? We will never know. And the world is now living with the terrible consequences.

When someone asks me what I want to hear first, the good news or the bad news, I always prefer the bad news first. If there's a problem, I want to start working on a solution immediately.

So, here are some bad news stories—and how I managed them as a "lanager." A "lanager" is a term coined by American business author and speaker Suzy Welch. It denotes the skill of having different combined attributes in business: You need to be a leader who inspires. And you need to be an effective manager who is close to the day-to-day workings of the company and focussed on details. I can't say that I was always the best "lanager." Sometimes, I did remove myself from the business and let others make the decisions. But when it came to dealing with a big crisis, I jumped in to solve it in a calm, practical manner.

Here's an example. In late May 1986, Phoenix Continental, our liability insurance provider, abruptly told us that our policy would be cancelled on June 8, even though it wasn't due to expire until August 1. This amounted to fifteen days' notice that AMJ Campbell, the largest independent moving company in Canada, with thirty-five locations and $60 million in annual business and more than one hundred trucks on the road, would have no liability coverage. A big, bad moment, indeed.

Admittedly, we'd been filing too many claims and needed to reduce our number of serious accidents per year. The moving business is not without catastrophes. We had a truck roll over on the 401, causing all the furniture to be strewn over the highway. One time, a driver of a tractor-trailer in Ottawa got distracted as he drove down a ramp on a steep embankment, resulting in a tragic accident that killed a woman and left her child with permanent injuries. That story hit the front page of *The Vancouver Sun* with our truck front and centre and the headline, "Horrific Crash."

We had strict safety rules, but our record was not perfect. And this policy change from our insurance provider was highly unfair, a shift that could sink any business, particularly a transportation business. Our competitors likely had a healthy dose of *schadenfreude* (pleasure over someone else's misfortune—in this case, ours). A headline in the *Toronto Star* from July 30, 1986, summarized it aptly: "Van Line Almost Ruined by Insurance Panic."

By that time, I had struck a partnership with Larry Papernick, a chartered accountant who played a substantial role in plotting the direction of AMJ Campbell. For several years, Larry had been our company auditor. When we were expanding briskly, he helped us refocus our controls and reporting structures. By the mid-1980s, I offered Larry a whopping 24 percent of the company in exchange for him becoming vice-president and chief financial officer. Although I'd remain the largest shareholder, with about 40 percent, my brothers Ted and Terry, who held roughly a combined 30 percent, were apprehensive about me giving up so much equity to one partner. But I was adamant. Larry worked hard seven days a week. He was a brilliant accountant with a sharp financial mind. He helped the company in myriad ways. But at times he would panic and get overly agitated about business issues.

That became clear over the insurance crisis—and others that I will explain later in this chapter. With the insurance problem, we came within a few weeks of being forced out of business and having to lay off 350 employees.

I had many sleepless nights during the two-week crisis while we fruitlessly hunted for a new insurer. As with many other companies, we were suddenly facing exorbitant liability insurance premiums.

But I didn't panic. Larry, however, did.

Throughout the crisis, he came whirling into my office. "What are we going to do?!" he fretted, caught up in a tailspin.

"Just relax," I said. I have never seen the value of panic. I can only make good decisions when I am calm. "We'll deal with it. It's not a problem," I said.

In fact, it was a problem, though not one without a solution. Perhaps because of my "lunatic years" with TC Moore when I seemed to encounter one stumbling block after another, I knew that solutions can be found if you take the time to look for them.

And we did find a solution.

We had three brokers working for us. They approached twenty-five or thirty insurance companies. Our options were few, and it took us until the final day of our termination notice to find an insurer, Guardian Insurance. Guardian was the only company that offered us coverage. Not surprisingly, the terms were steep: a 500 percent increase in our premium, from $110,000 to $550,000. The new policy tightened our cash flow significantly, but we were still in business.

By the end of the 1980s, AMJ Campbell was so successful, we had prospective buyers coming out of the woodwork. We were approached by Vector Inc., a Toronto investment firm, and Larry and I convinced my brothers and the other shareholders to sell majority control of the business.

This decision would lead to another crisis. But at the time, there were a couple of factors behind my decision to sell control of the company.

First, my mom had died in 1986, and her passing caused me to examine my priorities. I was in my mid-forties and had spent the past decade working nearly non-stop in transforming AMJ Campbell from a regional mom-and-pop moving company into a national powerhouse that was competing with the big American van lines. Part of me wanted to scale back my hours and involvement in the company. And unsurprisingly, Bernardine felt the same way. She longed to move back to the Maritimes.

Furthermore, the Vector deal held major advantages for AMJ Campbell and its shareholders. Under the terms of the sale, Vector secured 70 percent ownership of the company in exchange for $7 million, which valued AMJ Campbell at $10.5 million—a huge leap from the $50,000 Rick Renaud and I had paid for the original MJ Campbell in 1977. With the sweep of a pen, I greatly reduced my own financial risk and received a handsome payout.

Each part-owner received $110,000 per share, with most having only paid $5,000 to $15,000 per share, depending on when they had invested in the company. That meant my payout was $2.5 million; Larry's was $1.5 million; Ted, who died tragically about ten years later, got $1.5 million; and Terry got $1 million. Financially, it was not a difficult decision. I retained a 9.5 percent stake in AMJ Campbell—worth about $1 million—making me the largest shareholder after Vector.

For Vector, the deal's appeal was clear: we were reliably profitable (profits of $2.5 million on sales of nearly $40 million) and had demonstrated our hunger to expand across Canada and challenge the existing players in the industry. As Vector chair Albert Gnat told *Canadian Business* at the time, "[Vector] is not in this for a quick flip. We want to add value and we want to build AMJ Campbell into the premier moving company in the country."

Vector's financial muscle became apparent in January 1989, when Albert and I and Larry Papernick negotiated the purchase of Toronto-based CP Moving Systems, the $13 million household moving division of Canadian Pacific, which immediately expanded our jurisdiction into new centres in the Maritimes and Newfoundland and Labrador.

Vector had a very well-connected board, filled with business leaders who had reach into the corporate world. Among others, Ben Swirsky, then-president of Bramalea; Wayne MacLeod, president of CCL Industries; Alan Horn, president of Rogers Communications; Tony Griffiths, chair of Mitel; John Tory, blueblood lawyer and future Toronto mayor; Bill Estey, a former Supreme Court of Canada justice; and K. Rai Sahi, who was then an executive at the Bank of Montreal and now heads Morguard Corporation, a huge Mississauga-based real estate company with nearly $18 billion in assets owned or under management as of 2024.

In just the first six weeks of Vector ownership we added an astounding $2 million in new business thanks to those links with other Canadian companies. By 1990, our annual revenue had climbed to over $100 million.

The Vector deal also revealed, once again, the complacency and entitlement of the established players in the moving industry. In 1984, when *Canadian Business* interviewed Richard Shirk, president of North

American Van Lines, which was owned by PepsiCo, he brushed the deal aside and denied that it made us more threatening to his business. "[Shirk] concedes that Moore and his partners are 'good, tough competitors, excellent marketing people.' But he doubts that they could turn AMJ into a full-fledged [rival of the US-based] van lines because that would require massive expansion to give the company coverage in all major population centres."

In the end, though, we did just that.

Soon after the deal closed, I began working part-time on the East Coast, commuting regularly between Chester, NS, and Toronto. As I retreated, Larry's role within the company grew, so it seemed like an ideal time to shift my attention away from AMJ Campbell. The responsibility for achieving the growth to move AMJ Campbell into the big leagues no longer resided with me. It was Larry's. He was the new company president.

I agreed to stay under contract for two years to aid that transition. After a year, however, I asked for permission to leave early. The board—confident in Larry's abilities to carry on without me—allowed me to depart a year early.

At the time, whether because of naiveté or inexperience, it all seemed so simple. I'd exit the company while remaining a shareholder and get to enjoy my new life in Chester, confident in the sustained success of the business. Meanwhile, Larry would have the opportunity to lead the company his way, unencumbered by my presence. Larry was a smart, personable, and hard-working partner. I tend to think of myself as more of a survivor, more of a driver, having started on the street and suffered setbacks.

Far from simple, that arrangement turned out to be very complicated indeed.

Economic forces played a part in why this plan didn't work. First was the severe Canadian recession of the early 1990s. Second was Vector's decision—led by Chair Albert Gnat—to buy A&A Records, which, twenty years earlier, had been the dominant record store chain in Canada before the expansion of Sam the Record Man. Albert, apparently wanting to recapture A&A's past glory, hatched a plan to open one hundred new A&A stores—in one year! I was stunned. And my opinion hasn't changed. Without a war chest of unlimited funds, it was a recipe for disaster. When A&A collapsed in bankruptcy a year later, Vector lost a whopping $17 million.

But some of the problems facing AMJ Campbell lay with Larry, especially his penchant for leasing equipment instead of buying it outright. I am a big believer in paying cash for things whenever possible, especially small items. Under his leadership, the company was managing and paying for more than five dozen leases, covering everything from cars to trucks to phones—even $300 fax machines. Larry also didn't believe in getting out of obligations to the bank. I had always felt the opposite. I wanted to avoid using the bank's money if I could. But very quickly, Larry added heavily to our line of credit. Over the course of a year, he purchased a whole fleet of vans for the commercial department. And the leases kept mounting. He didn't adjust to the time with the recession.

There I was, with one foot in the company and the other planted 1,800 kilometres away in Chester. I was continually bombarded by phone calls and messages from people within the company, many asking me to intervene or fix some issue. One time, I had to jump on a plane to sort out a problem with a move for CN. A trailer full of the company's furniture had been parked in the yard in Montréal, scheduled to be driven out the next day. But someone jumped the truck and stole it. Later, it was found in northern Quebec, the whole thing burned. Other times, employees would call to tell me stories of ridiculous waste and overspending, which also required my intervention.

"If I had known what it was going to be like, we might as well have stayed in Toronto," Bernardine grumbled to me at one point. She was right. This was not a way to enjoy our life in Chester. Nor was it an effective way to help the business I still had a vested interest in.

The breaking point came in the spring of 1991, when I learned that the company's line of credit had ballooned to $4.5 million and, even worse, that AMJ Campbell, a reliably profitable company, had lost more than $2 million in the first five months of the year.

It was another crisis.

And there was more.

Along with some of the Vector board members, I met with TD Bank, hoping to boost our line of credit from $4.5 million to $6.5 million. The bank, already burned by the A&A Records debacle, was hesitant, only agreeing to the increase if we personally infused $1 million into the company.

I was not going to do that. I had sold my controlling interest.

What I would do, I said, was return full-time as chief executive for a two-year period. Larry would be demoted from president back to senior vice-president. That was a difficult conversation. I told him that I was sorry things had worked out this way. He hadn't done a terrible job. He had taken on too much debt. I said we would work together to turn things around. I wasn't mean about it. The recession was taking its toll, and the necessary adaptations to the economic conditions hadn't come fast enough. He was understandably hurt, but he anticipated that something drastic had to happen.

My decision was calm and came with strict conditions. Once again, I was taking the bull by the horns. Finding a solution and acting on it fast.

I wanted to switch all AMJ Campbell's small branches to a franchise model, cut twenty-five people from head office as well as overhead, and, of course, quickly wrestle the company's debt under control. Albert figured the board would agree to all my requests.

One hurdle remained: I had to convince Bernardine.

She was not surprised and not overly enthusiastic either. But when she knew something had to be done, she always sided with me. In short order, she found us a house in Burlington, a community in the Greater Toronto Area, west of the city centre.

She stepped up and supported me without rancour.

One of the most powerful lessons I've learned in fifty years of business is this: When you sign the cheques, you know what's happening within your business. After two years away from day-to-day operations, I jumped fully into the nitty-gritty details of AMJ Campbell's financial position and its spending.

Every two weeks I'd find a pile of cheques on my desk for signing. Sometimes, the pile was a foot high. I personally signed every cheque and could see every item we were paying for. And much of it was questionable. Flipping through the pile, I recall saying to myself, "There's all kinds of shit going on here." The most egregious finding was credit card abuse by some of our thirty- six delivery van drivers who, when stopping for gas, were adding drinks, food, and cigarettes to the fuel bill.

I also got us out of as many money-draining leases as possible and informed the entire company that spending would be restricted to items of absolute necessity: no more trucks and equipment purchases, no more office renovations, and no more large advances for drivers. Our spending had to be limited to priority items. Our payroll was also bloated and in need of a trim across every department.

It's never pleasant to dismiss employees, especially not in a company like AMJ Campbell that had built such a warm and inclusive culture. But I had some experience with this unpleasant task. Every year, during our years of growth in the 1980s, I would let roughly 10 percent of employees go due to inadequate performance in sales or administration or because their personality wasn't a good fit. In making those decisions, I would observe people, listen to feedback from colleagues, and then address the employees themselves, asking how they felt about their job. When I decided to fire someone, I invited them into my office, sat them down and explained that I was sorry things didn't work out. I pointed out problems with their performance, hoping to help them gain insight into themselves. Other times, it was simply a matter of needing to cut costs. But I never shirked the face-to-face explanations. Letting people go is a little bit of an art. You have to do it thoughtfully but directly and with sensitivity.

And you have to be prepared not to be liked, to have enemies, even. I had a few. You can't run a huge company and have everybody like you.

I discovered upon my return to the Toronto office that the company was paying about twenty-five underperformers, representing about 25 percent of our head office staff. They had to go. Two of the people I had to fire were family members. This was a sensitive issue. My priority was to maintain good relationships with both of them. I cared about them and the cohesion of our extended family. But I couldn't keep on people who weren't producing and were not particularly well suited to the task. I sat down with each and explained that their sales figures weren't strong enough. I pointed out their strengths and said I would give them good references. Handling such situations takes equal amounts of straightforward communication, compassion, and sensitivity.

The cuts troubled many of our employees, but I told them: "If you're doing your job, then you need not be worried." Senior managers, meanwhile, questioned me about the specifics of who I planned to let go. But I sidestepped those queries because I wanted to avoid favouritism and the office politics that could arise if the list was known ahead of time. One of the casualties was a twenty-year-veteran of the company, a man with lots of valuable experience in the moving business, though his attitude was temperamental and he was often curt with his co-workers. Some of my colleagues openly questioned my decision to let the man go while at the same time retaining a much younger employee in the same department. My answer: I'd rather have a positive person with less experience than a highly experienced employee with a bad attitude or sour personality. Especially during downtimes, you want employees with positive attitudes. Negativity is contagious and will hurt the company.

The only mistake I made in handing out that slew of terminations was letting an eighty-five-year-old warehouse worker go. He was sleeping every day on a sofa. My decision was justified—but not thoughtful. We weren't paying him much, and our company was part of his life. I quickly changed my mind and reinstated him. Sometimes, in life and in business, you have to change your mind and do something that might seem illogical. Many employees came to me after and expressed gratitude that I had continued this old codger's employment.

Around this time, Albert Gnat was replaced as Vector board chair by Arthur Walker, the former CEO of Algonquin Mercantile Corporation, a publicly traded company. Arthur proved to be a true asset to the company, especially during this time of cuts and restructuring. He was more hands-on than Albert and became both a friend and mentor to me.

Larry resigned in April 1992, shortly after Arthur's arrival.

Despite the cuts, layoffs, and spending freeze, we still posted a loss of $700,000 in 1992. Yet the company had survived, weathered the recession, and was on improved financial footing.

Still, further changes were needed—fundamental changes to how we ran the company. Over the next seven years, we franchised our many company-owned offices, a time-consuming endeavour that was essential to our long-term survival.

In my experience, franchising appeals to the conservative entrepreneur. They get the excitement and freedom of owning their own venture, combined with the support and security of a larger umbrella corporation. In other words, they are an owner, but they aren't alone in their venture.

Most of our franchisees were already branch managers, meaning they knew the workings of their operations very well. This lowered their risk even more. Within the franchisee model's blend of risk and security, they thrived.

But some were suspicious.

"Do I have to buy my job?" David Way, the manager of the Edmonton branch, asked me derisively. He thought that head office had "some kind of ulterior motive" in encouraging its managers to become franchisees.

I assured him that we would find him another position within the company if he decided not to buy the Edmonton branch. A month later, however, he'd completely changed his opinion of the franchise opportunity and paid $187,000 for his Edmonton branch.

David grew the Edmonton branch from fifteen people and four trucks in the mid-1980s to fifty people and fifteen trucks. In 1986, revenue was $1.1 million. By 1995, it had grown to $2.5 million. David was making more than $200,000 a year, way up from the $60,000 he'd been earning as a branch manager. Five years after buying the branch, he had tripled his earnings and took six weeks' vacation a year.

David eventually sold the Edmonton franchise and bought into our flagship Mississauga operation. His staff even developed their own slogan that applied to the whole AMJ Campbell family: Satisfied Employees Creating Unsurpassed Service.

David's experience was repeated throughout the company. Branch managers-turned-owners made more money, had more freedom, and could be more creative in catering to their local markets.

Essentially, it was the same principle that I'd used to revolutionize our industry when I put our drivers and packers on commission as independent contractors: a sense of ownership increases initiative, accountability, creativity, and profits. They can make more money. Some costs they can write off through their business. The packers and movers would also get bonuses based on feedback from customers.

For Vector, our majority owner, the benefits of franchising were many: less overhead, fewer administrative costs, the flow of royalties to head office, and no need to manage a network of satellite offices across the country, a time-consuming effort that involved stickhandling issues and claims from our head office. It was far more efficient to have a manager-turned-owner deal directly with those problems.

Personally, I had self-serving reasons for launching the franchise system. Before my semi-retirement and retreat to Chester, I'd essentially had no life outside of work. I was constantly busy—at all hours of the day and night—dealing with problems, accidents, claims, and hirings and firings across the country. Decentralizing all that responsibility was an enormous relief for me and my family.

To encourage our branch managers to buy their locations, we kept prices reasonable—often around three times a branch's annual earnings. We knew that each franchise had an increased chance of success if it was owned by the current manager. Bringing in outside owners—even if it brought better sale prices—would likely lead to many issues and franchise failures. Any reduction to the franchise fee was worth the stability and the increase in value that would be generated by profitable, manager-owned franchises. In other words, we knew that the right people would pay off in the long run, even if they paid less to get their franchise in the first place.

Our franchising push from 1992 until 1999 was incredibly time-consuming. We added franchises in North Bay, Sudbury, Timmins, and Thunder Bay in Ontario, as well as Fredericton and Saint John in New Brunswick. We even franchised a portion of our three largest centres: Calgary, Montréal, and Toronto, with all three locations posting record profits under the new arrangement. Before franchising, we were making somewhere between $50,000 and $100,000 from each of those locations. Within three years, though, Montréal generated a profit of more than $400,000; Calgary produced a $500,000 profit, and Toronto delivered a whopping $2.5 million in earnings.

There's perhaps no better way to convey the power of our franchise system than to highlight the story of Mike Savoy, one of my first employees, who worked his way up from mover to driver to franchise owner and, eventually, millionaire. Mike was still a teenager when I met him in Montréal in 1974. At the time, he had a choice: go on a trip to Europe with his friends or work for me for $4.50 an hour. He made the wise and enriching decision to join TC Moore Transport in Montréal, where he helped me move everything from tables and chairs to cabinets and pianos.

Following the sale of TC Moore, Mike followed me to AMJ Campbell and by the late 1970s he'd saved enough money to buy his own tractor-trailer. When he eventually tired of life on the road, he joined our operations department. In the early 1990s, he took a major risk by selling his house to finance the purchase of our St. Catharines franchise. Mike later bought the Halifax franchise and pushed sales to $2.4 million; a year later he secured a 50 percent interest in his hometown Montréal branch. Mike had been making around $60,000 a year in St. Catharines. By the late 1990s, he was earning a salary of $140,000, plus a bonus of $25,000, and dividends totalling $150,000. It was quite a rise for a guy who'd started lugging boxes for me as a teenager.

A true indication of our successful restructuring arrived in September 1992, when AMJ Campbell went public on the Toronto Stock Exchange, the first moving company to do so. It was a significant milestone for a company that, twenty years earlier, was only worth $50,000. Listed on the TSX as CamVec (a combination of Campbell and Vector, our major shareholder), the stock launched at $2 a share, quickly dropped, but later doubled and then quadrupled in value, to $8 a share.

By the spring of 1996, AMJ Campbell, excluding the franchisees, was doing more than $90 million in annual sales, had virtually no debt, and had $5 million in the bank.

We were on the move in more ways than one. But a serious roadblock lay ahead.

Chapter 7

Plan Your Succession and Don't Look Back

A leader's lasting value is measured by succession.

JOHN C. MAXWELL

Each time a man stands up for an ideal, or acts to improve the lot of others, or strikes out against injustice, he sends forth a tiny ripple of hope.

ROBERT KENNEDY

IN THE MID-1990s, THE VENERABLE CBC BROADCASTER PETER Gzowski interviewed me on his famous radio show, *Morningside*, about how I was able to run a national, Ontario-based company while living part of the year in a quaint seaside village in Nova Scotia. Peter, known colloquially as Captain Canada, had a folksy charm about him and could easily engage people in conversation on the radio. His listening audience was enormous: almost half a million people. He could make anyone feel at home, as though chatting in person over coffee in a sunlit kitchen. People would divulge their stories, illuminating their lives in whatever corner of Canada they inhabited.

As I did. Not regrettably, but maybe a bit too confidently. With supreme brio, I explained that I had returned to Chester for part of the year, having done my duty as CEO to resurrect AMJ Campbell during a difficult recession: trimmed costs, implemented the national franchise system, and reduced our debt to essentially zero. The company had millions in the bank, and I was nearly at the end of the two-year agreement that had brought Bernardine and me back to Mississauga in 1992, after agreeing to come out of semi-retirement.

I could do it all, I intimated. I could handle large claims from my office overlooking the sea. I could bring in big contracts through my network. I could handle management issues with a phone call. I could hop on a plane to Toronto if needed. I was still on the road for three months of the year, travelling for business. But I was happiest in my home office, I told him, convinced that I knew my business so well that I didn't need to be at the headquarters in Toronto all the time.

The only downside, I added jokingly, was that Bernardine had a habit of serving me hot cups of tea every twenty minutes. (With the occasional scone.) After the interview, we were swamped with calls from friends across the country who'd listened to the episode. Many couldn't believe that I'd taken a dig at my wife on national radio. Who wouldn't want tea served to them? Several asked if they could book a tea date with Bernardine at our house! She had earned collateral fame!

But the reality was that working remotely was not ideal. This was well before working remotely was in vogue—and before the Covid pandemic led to the technology that made it easier. But even now I would argue that something gets lost in communication when you only meet on Zoom. People pick up a lot of nuance and silent body language when they're sitting across a table from one another.

I was spinning a yarn in that radio interview with Peter. Or maybe I was just delusional to believe that I could still be a strong manager even while away from our head office for long stretches of time. I was not being truthful with myself about the future of my involvement with the company and how I could ease myself out and hand it off to a successor in an orderly manner.

Anne M. Mulcahy, the former CEO and chairwoman of Xerox, once said that succession planning "should be gradual and thoughtful, with lots of sharing of information and knowledge and perspective, so that it's almost a non-event when it happens."

This chapter is a cautionary tale. Succession planning is a crucial part of any business and entrepreneurial endeavour. We can't run the companies we founded forever. I freely admit that I did not manage the transition of mine in a well-thought-out manner. I want to clarify some of what happened in the hope that my story offers some lessons to those who are approaching this stage of their company's evolution.

Feel free to take notes.

Truth is, I had been wanting to step away from the company for some time. I didn't agree with some of the decisions of Arthur Walker, chair of CamVec, AMJ Campbell's parent company. By the spring of 1996, AMJ was doing $75 million in annual sales, and Arthur wanted to put some of that capital to work. He pushed for CamVec to buy Kord Products Limited, a $100-million specialty plastics and packaging company that served the medical, pharmaceutical, and horticultural sectors, and had $41 million in assets. But it hadn't been profitable in the previous five years.

I was skeptical of the Kord deal from the beginning, but I felt pressure to support it at the board level because Arthur was passionate about it. He'd been a valued supporter of mine since his addition to the board. I felt I owed him my allegiance in return.

Only one member of the board voted against the Kord purchase, and his no vote proved correct. By 1997, Kord had failed financially for two consecutive years, a trend that would continue. I was deeply disappointed in this.

Without any warning or even a hint to Arthur, I sold all my AMJ company shares when the stock was trading around $7.50 per unit. The Kord debacle was dragging the stock down. I wanted out. But even though I'd sold my equity interest in AMJ Campbell, I felt a moral and financial obligation to identify the best executive to take my spot.

The company's number-two executive, Chief Operating Officer Bruce Bowser, was expecting to be the new CEO. To any outside observer, it would have seemed a logical decision. It's common for a COO to eventually replace the CEO. And Bruce was someone I had mentored. But by that time, I had some hesitation over whether he was ready to be CEO.

I had first met Bruce in the early 1990s and hired him in 1992 to work in our logistics division. A year or two later, I provided an opportunity for him to buy a 22 percent stake in our Mississauga branch. He had shown good progression in terms of his day-to-day duties. I subsequently gave him an important assignment: the merger of our household goods and commercial divisions. Those two entities had been running as separate departments, but the crunch of the recession forced us to seek savings by combining them. Bruce succeeded in merging the household goods and commercial moving departments. He reshaped the divisions by bringing in some new people from outside the moving industry, empowering his staff to make decisions, increasing accountability, and reducing waste. Through a series of promotions, Bruce rose quickly to executive vice-president and chief operating officer.

But for a number of reasons, I was dragging my feet over appointing Bruce as my successor. As many business experts have pointed out, being a good manager or executive doesn't necessarily mean they're a shoo-in for CEO. That role requires vision, a strong work ethic, creativity, and excellent interpersonal skills—leadership qualities, in other words. And sometimes, those take time for someone to develop.

I had observed that Bruce's manner with people was sometimes unsatisfactory. I had also heard reservations about Bruce from senior partners within our current company.

I looked for other candidates. Twice, I tried to convince my brother Terry to step in as CEO, but he and his family had no interest in moving from Calgary to Mississauga. I pursued two other top candidates. But neither one of these possibilities worked out.

By early 1999, I was in a tough spot: My recruitment efforts had failed, and Arthur saw Bruce as my likely successor. I had two options: Negotiate a severance package and depart permanently for Chester (with Bruce taking my place), or let Bruce go, move back to Mississauga full-time, and recommit to being CEO until I could find a satisfactory replacement.

For Bernardine, however, the second option was nearly beyond consideration. She did not want to move back to Ontario. I felt that our family had made enough sacrifices over the years—Bernardine, especially. Moving households is not easy with children to raise. And frankly, after years of commuting between Chester and Mississauga, I was exhausted. I didn't want to move back to Ontario full-time either. I wanted to be in Chester.

Looking back, I feel that the succession plan was flawed from the outset. I thought then it was the right thing to do, but on reflection now, I realize it was destined to fail. I negotiated an exit package of a five-year consulting position at $150,000 a year with the title of advisory chair.

Bruce would replace me as chief executive, and I'd largely retreat to Chester, although I'd be available to smooth the transition and would maintain an office at AMJ Campbell headquarters in Mississauga. This was an arrangement made with Arthur, the chairman, not with Bruce. If I were in Bruce's position, I wouldn't have liked the former CEO and founder of the company looking over my shoulder. But I didn't have the wisdom of that perspective at the time.

I took Bruce aside and emphasized the golden position he had before him. At year-end on March 31, 1999, AMJ Campbell posted an operating profit of $4.7 million on $53 million in sales, which excluded the $65 million in sales achieved by our thirty franchisees. Our closest competitor in Canada was selling $60 million below us. I was leaving the company in great shape.

"This is an opportunity of a lifetime," I told him. "Don't blow it."

I knew that his management style would be different than mine—that was to be expected. There are many different types of successful managers. There's no one correct way to inspire and lead. I merely wanted him to consider ways that he could improve and grow into the position. If that sounds pedantic on my part, well, it was. Maybe I was still thinking of myself as his mentor. I thought my guidance was important even though I was essentially leaving the company.

In September 1999, Bruce was appointed president of AMJ Campbell. A year later, the board elevated him to CEO. Bruce obviously didn't want my input. He never sought me out for help or counsel in my role as advisory chair. I was also supposed to serve as an ambassador of sorts for the company, including by attending AMJ Campbell's annual conventions. Bruce, however, didn't want me at those functions. I can understand why. He was the CEO. He wanted to run the place and didn't feel he needed me. Our succession plan was not well thought out.

As it turned out, the succession plan that was supposed to ease the transition made it difficult. It created discomfort and resentment—not the feelings you want in a period of change. I was barely out the door of AMJ Campbell's head office when photos of our national partners and key people in the company's history, like salesperson extraordinaire Jackie Stewart, were removed from the lobby and boardroom walls. I can only assume it was intended to wipe the company's history aside and signal a new chapter. But it felt disrespectful of the success the company had built.

My feelings of regret over my bungled departure from AMJ Campbell are tempered somewhat by a gift I received from Arthur Walker in December 1998: a heavy steel sculpture by Boris Kramer called *The Achiever*, which is meant to represent "the triumph of determination in order to overcome the challenges of life." With it was a handwritten note:

Dear Tim,
For Christmas this year, I felt it important that you should have this Kramer creation because it speaks to me of so much that is you.

In the forging process something striking is made to rise from the humblest of raw materials to take on its own unique shape in the skillful forger's hands. As is the case in life, a limited few of such creations emerge above and beyond others to become "Achievers"—cured in the crucible of life—made hard and strong by day-by-day experiences—and finally burnished and polished to reflect the striking brilliance of the Great Refiner's fire!

May you find pleasure, Tim, in this particular creation—and may its symbolism be both meaningful as well as inspiring to you as a friend who to me is one of Life's very special "Achievers."

With warm affection
Arthur

Arthur's letter is among the nicest things I've ever received during my business career. The Kramer sculpture still stands prominently in my home office with the letter framed nearby.

Arthur passed away shortly after giving me this touching gift, and it comforts me to know that despite all the chaos of those final years working together we were still friends who respected and appreciated each other.

I see now that I should have taken my retirement package, left the company entirely, and never looked back. I should have followed the advice of cable TV mogul John Malone, the "Cable Cowboy," who sold his company, Telecommunications Inc (TCI), to AT&T in 1999 for US$48 billion. He cashed out at its peak "When you sell, sell!" he later counselled. "Get out!"

But I was not out, not contractually and certainly not emotionally. From roughly 2000 to 2003, I was contacted often by AMJ Campbell employees and franchisees who wanted to vent their frustrations and concerns about the company's direction and leadership. It was an awkward position for me to be in. Most often, I would encourage them to go to Bruce to explain their point of view and find solutions. Some employees were very close to me; I considered them my friends, as they had worked as part of the team for many years. One, who knew me well, didn't hesitate to communicate her dismay.

"Tim, you gotta get me out of here," she told me in 2003. "I'm ready to go pour coffee at Tim Hortons."

It appeared to me that the company culture we'd thoughtfully built over the course of decades—the culture that was responsible for so much of our repeat business and high company morale—was changing. A company that had been run collaboratively, with a great deal of decision-making power given to the franchise owners—the people who knew their individual markets best—was now increasingly being run from the top down. Plus, AMJ Campbell had lost several valuable contracts—two being with CBC and CN—and our profitability and share price were dropping.

I tried to intervene and help, but I was told to back off and mind my own business. In October 2002, I was informed that my consulting contract would be terminated if I didn't butt out. But that didn't scare me.

"I'm not going to prostitute myself for money," I told Bernardine. "I don't need the money that badly."

Feeling ignored and fearful for the direction of the company and its employees, I penned a letter to Bruce—only to Bruce—dated December 8, 2002. I told him I was there to help: "I know that you have a distaste for my writing you letters but it seems that it's the only way that I can formalize my thoughts and have them listened to without disagreement or confrontation."

Well, my letter exacerbated the tensions. Bruce shared the letter with new AMJ Campbell chair, Wayne McLeod, and the pair quickly cancelled my advisory contract.

I didn't regret writing that letter. I felt that it was my fiduciary duty as advisory chair (and moral duty as founder) to express my concerns. I was no longer CEO or even a shareholder but—for better and for worse—I remained emotionally connected to AMJ Campbell.

For many entrepreneurs, their company is like their offspring. You give birth to it. Nurture it. Discipline it. Watch it grow. This was true for me. I cared deeply about it and its people (my friends!). And I had brought Bruce into AMJ Campbell in 1992 and given him a multitude of opportunities. This was my payback? I was shocked, insulted, and saddened. Was it a mistake to be so emotionally invested? Perhaps, but I couldn't help myself. I'd poured too much of myself into the company, and received too much in return, to stand by as its culture lost the verve that had made AMJ Campbell a huge success.

Terry was equally troubled and, like me, put his concerns in writing. Despite running a powerhouse operation and proving himself a top operator in North America, he was rebuffed and treated like a junior employee.

But Terry was not your average owner. Over a twenty-year period, he had increased revenues and profits every year (with the exception of a single year), and Calgary's household goods division often produced bigger profits than that of Mississauga, the company's largest branch. For two consecutive years between 2000 and 2002, Terry's Calgary branch was Atlas's number one cross-border agent. In 2002, the Calgary branch was named Atlas's Agent of the Year in Canada, with net revenue of $4.5 million, beating out 160 other agents across the country.

As Terry wrote in an email to Bruce and the board of directors in the spring of 2001: "AMJ Calgary has constantly been one of the most successful moving companies in North America.... Despite the successes for the past two years I sincerely feel that it is your intent to rid yourself of another part of the history of this organization, namely myself," Terry wrote.

Turned out he was right. Soon after, Terry learned from an insider that he was going to be fired.

He was tipped off that someone was coming to Calgary to officially boot him out. There was no courteous phone call from Bruce to say his termination was about to happen and to explain the reasons. On March 10, 2003, after twenty-three years of outstanding success in building our Western Canadian business from nothing, Terry was kicked out of the company. In my view, there are appropriate and professional ways of ending someone's employment, especially for senior partners of high performance who have a long history with the company. As further insult, Terry was immediately asked for the keys to his car.

Terry and I both sued Bruce and AMJ Campbell for wrongful dismissal and ultimately settled out of court. Both of us wanted to avoid a protracted battle and simply move on to new ventures, not waste money on lawyers.

Shortly after leaving AMJ Campbell, Terry got a call from the owner of King's Transfer Moving & Storage in Montréal, asking if he'd join as the company's representative in Western Canada. He'd be given full control to grow King's Transfer in the West. And he did just that with King's Transfer Van Lines, building in seven years what had taken twenty years to create with AMJ Campbell. (Many AMJ Campbell employees jumped ship to work with Terry at King's Transfer.) Terry was a wealth of knowledge and experience, and King's Transfer benefitted from both. (In 2024, Terry was honoured at the AMJ Campbell annual convention, a well-deserved recognition of his huge contribution to the company. Unfortunately, it was twenty years late, though the gesture was appreciated.)

Terry and I were not alone in leaving AMJ Campbell in 2003. Seventeen disgruntled AMJ Campbell franchisees left the organization in the wake of these management changes. But they weren't deterred. Instead, they planned to launch their own moving company—a rival to mighty AMJ Campbell. And they asked me to help, even though I had moved on to other entrepreneurial pursuits at the time.

Then, in late 2004, the company went private. With the disaster of the Kord purchase, the stock had fallen at one point to as low as fifty cents. The board approved a management takeover offer organized by Bruce and the Frappier group, comprising several members of the Frappier family who had become part of the company over time. They were excellent operators and knew how to make money.

Ironically, this difficult period in the proud company's history happened shortly after the Canadian Association of Movers had honoured me with their distinguished service award, recognizing my many years in the industry.

In November 2004, I met with the seventeen franchisees who'd decided to depart AMJ Campbell at the Marriott hotel in Toronto, and I outlined my plan. In some capacity, I'd worked with every person in the room. I wanted to talk to them from the heart. I congratulated them on their courage and unwavering resolve through the process and rallied them on the idea of a new van line, which I committed to helping to run for two years. The new moving company would be communally owned (the franchisees would hold 80 percent; I'd own 20 percent), and, of course, it would be dedicated to the trademark quality service that was at the core of AMJ Campbell. In April 2005, Premiere Van Lines, founded by me and the breakaway AMJ franchisees, was launched.

Bruce claimed that I was motivated by ego. "The company [AMJ Campbell] is a lot bigger than Bruce Bowser and Tim Moore. I understand that. I'm not sure Tim does," Bruce told *allNovaScotia*. "Tim has not been a shareholder in AMJ to any degree for seven, eight, nine years. It's hard when the founder of the company can't let go."

Needless to say, the media gobbled up the news.

"The announcement came dripping with irony: Moore would take up the lance against his former protégé, Bruce Bowser," noted an article in the *Mississauga Business Times*. "Forget irony, Moore's Premiere venture [is] getting downright personal, right? It's a charge he thoroughly denies. Still, industry insiders aren't buying it."

Then there was the lead sentence of a *Globe and Mail* article from February 7, 2005: "Tim Moore spent two decades building AMJ Campbell Inc. from a tiny [moving company] into Canada's biggest mover. But now he wants to run his old company off the road."

Both descriptions were exaggerations. I wasn't trying to destroy AMJ Campbell, and it wasn't a story of revenge. After leaving AMJ Campbell in late 2002—when my consulting contract was terminated—I had no intention of going back into the moving business. I was already deeply engaged in new ventures. But, simply put, I went back into the moving business out of respect for other people in the AMJ Campbell family. This was a story of loyalty—loyalty to the many AMJ Campbell owners who had helped me build the company into a national leader, but who I felt were now being treated unfairly.

Looking back, I'm still amazed at the reach and strength that Premiere Van Lines generated from its inception. The initial branches covered more than twenty cities, including St. John's, Halifax, Truro, Sydney, Moncton, Saint John, Fredericton, Sherbrooke, Mississauga, Scarborough, Kitchener, St. Catharines, London, Windsor, Thunder Bay, Winnipeg, Regina, Saskatoon, Medicine Hat, Calgary, Vancouver, and Dallas, Texas.

Premiere Van Lines boasted more than $40 million in revenue right out of the gate, making us—overnight—the second-largest moving company in Canada, behind only AMJ Campbell. By comparison, AMJ Campbell's fifty locations across Canada had previously produced annual sales of $130 million. In the space of nine months, we had about twenty-five offices in twenty-two cities and towns across Canada.

Unfortunately, I suffered a minor heart attack in 2005, which forced me to depart as CEO after only about sixteen months in the job, cutting short my two-year commitment. But I don't regret starting the company. And I'm proud of the chutzpah and energy of my partners. In the end, Premiere Van Lines failed to grow to a size rivalling AMJ Campbell. Today, the company still has offices from coast to coast and its ranks include many of my former AMJ Campbell colleagues. Premiere Van Lines provided a bright, encouraging conclusion to what could have been a very disheartening end to my career in the moving business. It was immensely satisfying to have my experience and knowledge appreciated by the company's founding franchisees.

Planning early is key to effective succession. And straightforward communication about how it will work is also important. A good example is the recent succession story at Walmart. In November 2025, Doug McMillon, Walmart CEO who was highly praised for modernizing the company into an e-commerce powerhouse in the age of AI, announced that he would be retiring effective late January 2026. This was a big deal. He is a transformational figure who had started his career at the company as a warehouse worker. Within ten years of his appointment as CEO, Walmart shares had risen 300 percent. But here's the good news. Walmart had planned their CEO succession well. They had discussed it at the Board level over the years. In fact, Doug would be stepping down from both the C-suite and the board, a move that suggested the high confidence level the company had in the change at the top. John Furner, who had a three-decade history with Walmart, stepped into the role. "This was a planned and thoughtful leadership transition from a position of strength," a Walmart spokesperson commented. Such leadership continuity is crucial to ensure investor confidence.

My lack of a solid and well-executed plan was exemplary for what not to do. My advice would be to work with an outside professional organization to negotiate and plan your exit. This may seem counterintuitive. You may think you know your company best and what it needs as a successor or what you should do to orchestrate your exit. But an outside professional removes the emotion from those decisions and will help the company plot the best future without you. They can also negotiate the best monetary exit package for you.

I hope your notebook is full with insights.

Happily, I hasten to point out that companies can bounce back from challenging periods. AMJ Campbell did. Bruce was CEO for twenty-three years, and by all accounts did a good job. According to Pierre Frappier, the sole owner of AMJ Campbell, Bruce chose not to have a contract when he sold his shares and decided to leave the company. Bruce told him he had learned a lesson from the debacle of my contractual arrangement. In 2025, Pierre invited me to their head office in Mississauga, Ontario. He gave me a tour around three buildings, introducing me to everyone as the founder. He had often shown respect for me in this way. AMJ had declined to charge me for some personal moves I had hired the company to do when Bernardine and I were relocating from some of our properties. I had insisted on paying them as planned. I always supported AMJ when I needed a mover. But out of deference to me as the founder, Pierre had instructed AMJ's sales representative to tell me the moves were complimentary. These acknowledgements of me as a valued ambassador were thoughtful and generous

In conclusion, as I look back, I always feel it's important in life and in business to not burn bridges. Bruce had his own style of management. It just wasn't mine. Change is the only constant. You have to deal with it. In 2020, Bruce and AMJ Campbell honoured me as the founder by giving me an original painting of our movers with an AMJ Campbell truck. I hung it in a prominent place in my home office. It was accompanied by a conciliatory note from Bruce, inferring that with age comes grace. I greatly appreciated that.

We all make mistakes. That's life. That's business. And it's important to reflect on the errors, learn, and move on. I believe that we both did. In the last few years, we have been cordial and respectful to each other.

Chapter 8

How to Make Money in Your Sleep

Real estate cannot be lost or stolen, nor can it be carried away. Purchased with common sense, paid for in full, and managed with reasonable care, it is about the safest investment in the world.

FRANKLIN D. ROOSEVELT

IN 1971, THE SAME YEAR THAT I TRADED MY VOLKSWAGEN FOR my second-hand Ford pickup truck, I borrowed $1,000 from a friend as a down payment on a $15,000 townhouse in the Dollard-des-Ormeaux area of Montréal West. I was nervous when I signed the papers on that first property. I was just starting out in my business. But I had a hunch about the value of real estate on Montréal's West Island. I could see that there was a lot of development going on in that part of the city. And I knew a rental fee could cover the mortgage. It's always smart to buy in a neighbourhood that's transitioning—not too fancy and not too derelict. Somewhere that's on the rise.

I like real estate for a simple reason. You can see it, touch it, and feel it. For years, it was my side hustle; my diversification strategy. I was making money in my sleep. I invested in many things as I grew wealthy: stocks, bonds, commodity futures, gold bars, precious gems. But nothing has made me more money than real estate. Which is not to say that I didn't have some duds. The condominium I lived in at Palace Pier on the Toronto waterfront cost me $450,000 when I bought it and dropped in value to about $300,000 in the 1990s recession. I know that now there's a lot of talk about the Canadian real estate market not being a slam-dunk investment anymore. The condo market in Toronto has cratered. But you have to play the long game with real estate. The value will increase over time. You can always rent it out. The Toronto market will come back. And when the market is down, it's a good time to buy at bargain prices.

When I started out, I had to identify good properties and find a reliable, trustworthy realtor who also had their ear to the ground for areas that were gentrifying and popular. You want to have someone keeping an eye out for you. I was a scavenger, always on the hunt for a good buy. And I had to be a shrewd negotiator. I've made more by buying low and selling high within two or three years than I would have if I'd paid market value and hung on to it for ten years, which is the term experts advise. It's about location and timing. I had to be ready to sell when the time was right.

Within a week, a real estate agent offered me $16,000 for that first townhouse—a nearly 7 percent increase over its purchase price. I turned it down because I knew it would only increase in value. Within two years, I sold it for $26,000—$11,000 more than I'd paid for it. I ended up buying and selling four four-plexes in LaSalle, Quebec, each costing between $35,000 and $40,000. I made around $10,000 to $15,000 on each one.

I'm not perfect; I did make some mistakes. Perhaps I got carried away in my real estate zeal. One was particularly laughable. I bought a small house near Dorval airport, having viewed it late at night. I thought it was a great investment. But the next week, I was walking through the house when it shook like it was at the epicentre of an earthquake. Yes. It was very close to the edge of a landing strip for that airport. It took me a year to unload that house, although I managed to break even on that sale. It was definitely a lesson in the importance of researching a home and neighbourhood in daylight, and in not making too hasty a decision! I also learned that when something is not working, cut our losses and get out.

By 1980, I'd cycled through more than a dozen properties and still owned five. I made it a (somewhat flexible) rule not to have more than six to eight properties at one time. Anything more was simply too much to handle. I didn't want to use professional property managers. I preferred to handle everything myself, including screening tenants.

That approach continued as I bought and sold more than forty properties between 1980 and the mid-1990s. I expanded my real estate holdings beyond Montréal, always following my tradition of offering what some sellers considered an "insulting" offer. I didn't care what they thought. That was my offer. One noteworthy deal was in Moncton, New Brunswick, Bernardine's hometown. A commercial property was asking $1.5 million. Soon, the price dropped to $900,000. The owners were struggling to sell it. I offered $600,000. The counter offer came in at $850,000. I declined. He got no other offers. Within a month, it was sold to me for $650,000. I subdivided the property, put $200,000 into it, and then sold it for $1.1 million. If they had held firm in the $800,000 range, I would have walked away. Timing and the willingness to hold out for a good deal combined for the winning strategy.

I bought recreational properties, including condos in Stowe, Vermont; Whistler, British Columbia; and Collingwood, Ontario. There were always people interested in renting a condo in a popular ski resort. My family could also use them for ski holidays. I let corporate clients use them. Those investments served many purposes.

I also employed my love of real estate for my moving business. In 1980, we bought our own building in Mississauga when most movers operated out of leased premises. That building, which was approximately 14,000 square feet, cost about $250,000. I sold it four years later for $450,000 as the area was going through a boom. That transaction and hefty profit helped me buy the four acres of land just west of the Toronto airport where we designed and built our legendary headquarters.

By 1999, Bernardine and I held a valuable real estate portfolio that included our waterfront house in Chester, some other houses in Chester, a few commercial buildings, and a Toronto condo.

Around this time was when I decided to dabble in the executive suites business. This was at the time when Bruce Bowser had become the CEO of AMJ Campbell, and I was phasing out. I wanted a new venture, and figured I'd start slowly. I bought a condo unit in Charter House, in downtown Halifax. I furnished it and placed an ad in the local paper for a short-term rental. Within a day or two I'd secured a one-year lease with a British oil executive who was working in Nova Scotia's offshore energy sector (a booming business at the time). That swift response convinced me to buy, furnish, and advertise a second unit in Charter House. It was quickly snapped up for a six-month lease.

So, I bought another one. And another. Before I knew it, I'd bought twenty-seven condos. In Halifax, I was fortunate to work with Sandra Bryant, the biggest realtor in the city. Throughout the years, I bought at least sixty properties through her firm, Bryant Realty Atlantic. Matthew, my son, was also instrumental in helping to scout good real estate deals.

My accountant, Terry Carter, was alarmed when I went on the condo spree in Halifax. But he didn't tell me of his concern until a year later. "I thought you were losing it," he confessed to me. By then, however, it was apparent that my gamble wasn't mere impetuousness or a sign of temporary insanity. It was a well-timed, instinctive bet on the Halifax real estate market, and it turned into my second national business: Premiere Executive Suites, an upscale extended-stay hospitality provider that eventually peaked with 1,200 units across six provinces and annual revenues of roughly $20 million. It remains today the largest extended-stay provider in Canada.

But at the beginning, I knew nothing about the suites business. What I had was a hunch that local real estate prices would soon explode, as well as a willingness to take a calculated risk.

At the time, a common refrain from naysayers was, "What if real estate prices drop?" With any business idea, there will be people who claim that you can't do it, or that you shouldn't do it. Don't be discouraged. Have your own mind and your own opinion. If you truly feel something is missing in the marketplace, don't be dispirited by doubters. No matter how lucrative an idea, there will always be someone declaring it a folly in the making. A big part of entrepreneurship is looking past that noise and putting your money on the line in support of your idea.

In the case of the suites business, I knew East Coast real estate prices would follow those elsewhere in Canada, and I wanted to get in the game before liftoff. I felt that would be especially true in Halifax, a growing city that hadn't yet experienced exploding real estate prices, such as in Toronto, Calgary, and Vancouver. I'd spent a lot of time in those markets, and I knew that real estate prices on the East Coast were too low and would eventually follow that upward trajectory. The result: I was buying condo units in 1999 for around $75,000 that tripled in value within ten years.

The suites model appealed to me for the same reason that I had started buying real estate in the 1970s. I could greatly expand my real estate holdings while funding that expansion with rental income. Even if I only broke even on the carrying costs, I'd come out ahead financially as the properties appreciated in value.

Initially, I figured I'd run a small, boutique-style accommodation business. But I continued to buy more and more units. I soon became overwhelmed by the work involved. "I realized after a month that I was in trouble," I told *Profit* magazine in 2003. "The demands of furnishing and maintaining twenty-eight units were unbelievable." I was essentially running a hotel, except with rooms spread across different buildings, and the stresses were the same: staff had to be friendly and responsive; repairs needed to be made within hours; housekeepers had to ensure each room was spotless—even after a guest had two weeks to mess it up.

Given my dedication to customer service at AMJ Campbell, I believed that if anyone could figure out what a suites customer needed, it was me. Nevertheless, during those early months I was constantly on the phone to Thom Vincent, a twenty-year acquaintance who'd built a large corporate-housing company in Toronto. He sold it in 1998 to Virginia-based Bridgestreet Corporate Housing Worldwide, which operated more than nine thousand executive apartments. He was the person who had started my interest in the suites business. I asked him a flurry of questions as I ramped up my understanding of the sector. I also asked David Morton, CEO of the Mac Group in Toronto about the industry, and he was happy to share his knowledge. Do you have a reservation system? How do you keep track of everything? How much do you pay your housecleaners? How often do you clean the rooms? Where do you get most of your business? What sites are best for getting business? Are there any issues with the condo buildings you're operating out of? When you know nothing, there's no such thing as a stupid question.

My solution in building Premiere Executive Suites was to return to the partnership playbook that I'd used in structuring AMJ Campbell: I needed smart, dedicated partners to join me as investors and operators. I didn't plan to expand outside of Halifax, but it happened, and I built the business with trusted partners. As I explained at the time: "I needed to line up friends and old AMJ franchisees to start buying condos with me in other cities—to put their money and asses on the line."

My first partnership target was Suzanne Bachur, a former AMJ Campbell employee who'd started as a receptionist in Mississauga in 1979. Suzanne had no formal training when I interviewed her, but she was enthusiastic, bilingual, had a glowing personality and a natural ability to communicate, and—as I later discovered—an aptitude for reading financials. I hired her immediately and she used all those skills to move up the ranks at AMJ Campbell, serving as claims manager, before leaving the company in the mid-1980s.

By 1999, I was already partnered with Suzanne and her husband, Ron, in two Swiss Chalet restaurants in Halifax—another side investment I had made, largely because I was a fan of Swiss Chalet food—so I knew she'd be a solid partner. Suzanne was skilled in promotional activities, customer relations, and in motivating staff members. I was sure that she'd be able to apply those skills to the suites business. The company also needed better structure. I was so busy buying real estate that I hadn't yet developed the documents needed for selling, leasing, and managing that real estate. We also needed a reservation system, a schedule for the cleaning staff, and dedicated accounting.

In May 1999, Suzanne listened to my pitch, and said she'd discuss it with Ron. The next day she called back: they were in. Suzanne and Ron bought a combined 15 percent of the business for $185,000. She quickly added that much-needed structure. This was the more formal launch of Premiere Executive Suites.

Executive apartments are often aimed at business people who don't need a permanent address, but who also don't want to shell out hotel-room rates for weeks or months on end. That segment of the market accounted for a large percentage of our business in all our venues. But there was a wide range of other clients. Insurance companies often send people somewhere for a few weeks or months when they have to move out of their homes due to floods or fires. Out-of-town parents with children in hospital need a comforting place to stay. People who have moved into town to take a new job often need a place to stay until they get established. Homeowners who were undertaking a large renovation needed a place to live while the work was under way. At one point, we signed a deal whereby Royal LePage's nine thousand real estate agents could refer relocating homebuyers to Premiere.

The appeal was straightforward: an extended-stay rental that's furnished and fully equipped with a kitchen, desk, parking, and housekeeping service. Available for rent by the month or sometimes by the week. Essentially, it's a home away from home.

All the suites were different designs with high-end furnishings, quality linens, flat-screen TVs, and special French shampoos, conditioners, and body creams in little bottles. In many of the units, we supplied Nespresso machines and Bose music systems. The staff, dressed in neat uniforms, acted like a concierge helping guests book restaurants and entertainment. They greeted customers on-site in order to make them feel at home and get to know them.

Tatiana Kredl, my partner in the Montréal operation of Premiere Executive Suites, captured the spirit of corporate housing well when she told the *Montréal Gazette* in 2004: "We give them a homey, cozy environment. That way, psychologically, employees [working on the road] feel looked after."

Our approach to pricing mirrored the strategy I had employed during my days as a one-truck mover in Montréal in the early 1970s. I purposely charged less than my competitors. In the beginning, we charged $1,300 a month for a 550-square-foot, fully equipped and furnished condo in Halifax. That came out to about $40 a night, considerably less than what was being charged by our competitors or by local hotels. This pricing strategy resulted in a higher occupancy ratio, which covered our costs and provided a profit. As our reputation for service grew, we were able to raise our rates to between $60 and $160 per night, depending on the type of unit, which ranged from bachelor apartments to townhouses.

The suites rental model was already well-established in Toronto but was less known and largely misunderstood on the East Coast. The novelty of our suites business can be seen in a *Frank* magazine article from December 2001, which ran under the headline, "Welcome to Tim Moore's Waterfront 'Hotel'!" In true *Frank* style, the article was featured under the magazine's "Worse Homes & Gardens" banner and was credited to the pseudonym "Belle Boye."

The "hotel" in question was Waterfront Place, a condominium complex in downtown Halifax where I'd "gobbled up" twenty one-bedroom units and was renting them for between $1,300 and $1,900 a month. As *Frank* noted, our Waterfront Place units (each about 550 square feet in size) were part of our larger roster of about a hundred units in and around Halifax, including at the former Queen Street Inn, a twelve-unit building we'd spent $250,000 renovating. Our revenue was expected to top $4 million in 2002, which *Frank* rightly described as "phenomenal growth," given that we'd only been in business for two years.

"But alas, not everyone at Waterfront Place is pleased with Tim's vision. Some owner/occupants at the posh downtown condo complex don't think they should be catering to the hotel trade—high end or not," the magazine noted.

These complaints were merely growing pains, and didn't linger beyond our first couple of years in business. Tenants in our buildings simply weren't familiar with the idea of extended-stay rentals, but they soon warmed to it—or at least accepted it.

Thankfully, the writers at *Frank* weren't alerted to one of my early gaffes in the suites business. It involved one of our first clients, a lovely woman who worked for Convergys, the insurance company, and who regularly rented a suite in downtown Halifax. One morning, she called me in a panic because she'd left her unit to grab the morning newspaper, and the door had closed and locked behind her. She didn't have a key and was dressed only in her negligee. This was not a scenario I'd planned for. There was a security desk at the time in the building but, unbelievably,

Tim Moore's parents, Tom and June Moore.

Tim Moore, second from right in the front row, with his father and siblings, ca. 1960s. Front row, from left: sister Bonnie; father, Tom; sisters Lynn and Anne. Back row, from left: brothers Terry and Ted.

Tim Moore, number 35, with his basketball team at Michael Power High School in Toronto, ON, ca. 1966. John Hunkin, who would go on to become president of the Canadian Imperial Bank of Commerce, is number 12.

Tim Moore with his mother, June, enjoying quality time on Bark Lake, QC, ca. 1950s.

Moore was a student at St. Augustine's Seminary of Toronto from 1967 to 1969.

Tim Moore, second from right, and his fellow seminarians at St. Augustine's.

Moore with his first delivery truck in Montréal, QC, in 1971.

Moore's first large moving truck, Montréal, ca. 1973.

The company's first van line truck, ca. 1979.

Breaking ground for the Mississauga office, 1984. From left: Tim Moore, Mississauga Mayor Hazel McCallion, and a representative of the construction company George Wimpey Canada.

The 75,000-square-foot AMJ Campbell Van Lines building in Mississauga, ON, in the early 1990s. The company was the official mover for both the Toronto Raptors and the Toronto Maple Leafs.

Matthew Moore, Tim's son, in Chester, NS, heading for Toronto with his first moving truck, ca. 1999.

Matthew Moore's first large truck, shown here in New York, NY, in 2001, shortly after 9/11.

Tim Moore, in the front row next to the woman in the white dress, with the senior partners from AMJ Campbell in Mississauga, ON, ca. 1987.

Tim Moore (front row, right) with partners from AMJ Campbell, ca. 1980. Rick Renaud is next to Tim in the front row.

Moore and biathlete Myriam Bédard at Canada House during the Winter Olympics in Lillehammer, Norway, in 1994.

Tim Moore with his siblings. Back row, from left: Ted (d. 2017), Terry, and Tim. Front row, from left: Lynn, Bonnie, and Anne.

Tim Moore, left, received Queen Elizabeth II's Golden Jubilee Medal in 2002. Next to him, from left: the Honourable Myra Freeman, Larry Freeman, and Bernardine Moore.

Bernardine and Tim Moore at the Crane Resort in Barbados, 2003.

Moore on a motorcycle excursion to Newfoundland and Labrador, ca. 2003.

Tim Moore, at left, with friends Albert Stadlin and Mike Flynn, during a motorcycle trip to the Cabot Trail in Nova Scotia, ca. 2005.

Tim Moore on a heli-skiing trip in the Bugaboos mountain range in British Columbia, ca. 2004.

Moore with his 1960 Rolls-Royce Silver Cloud, Mississauga, ON, ca. 1980s.

A charity event at the Moore home in Chester, NS, in 2009 raised more than $107,000 for the Stephen Lewis Foundation.

Two families joined. Tim Moore's son Chris (far right) is married to Lizzie Dodds (back row, left). In front of Lizzie, their two children, Victoria and William; continuing from left: Carol Dodds, Dr. Colin Dodds (former president of Saint Mary's University), Matthew, Tim, and Bernardine Moore.

Tim Moore and his son Chris in Nova Scotia's Annapolis Valley, ca. 2015.

Tim Moore and his son Matthew in Iceland, ca. 2016.

Granddaughter Katie's wedding in Montana in 2024. From left: Matthew, Tim, and Bernardine Moore, Katie Welch, Scott Welch, and Jason Moore.

Tim Moore received an honourary doctorate from Saint Mary's University in Halifax in 2016. From left: former chair of SMU's board of governors Bob Belliveau, Tim Moore, former SMU president Dr. Colin Dodds, and former board chair Paul Dyer.

At left, Tim and Bernardine Moore, and above, Terry and Tim Moore, during a heli-hiking trip in the Bugaboos mountain range in BC, ca. 2000.

Timmy and Jason Moore, Tim's "beautiful American boys."

Oceanstone Resort. [TIM L'ESPERANCE]

The Moore home in Chester, NS.

Bernardine and Tim Moore at their home in Chester, NS, in 2025.
[Sándor Fizli]

there was no spare key available. Thankfully, they soon changed this arrangement. But at the time, the only person with a spare key was me—in Chester. I set a new personal time record in making the sixty-five-kilometre drive to downtown Halifax and found her outside the unit, trying to conceal her skimpy clothing. I apologized. Fortunately, she had a sense of humour about the whole episode and continued to rent with us. Nevertheless, it was a reminder to ensure you've always got a backup plan in case a problem should occur.

By 2003, with a strong foothold established on the East Coast, I decided to expand Premiere Executive Suites into Toronto, believing there was still room for more competition in that market.

My first call was to Kim Boydell.

Kim's career can be summarized in five words: from the mailroom to millionaire. With only a high school diploma, she started in mailrooms, including at Kmart, before she joined AMJ Campbell in 1988 as a sales secretary at our head office in Mississauga. She eventually spent close to fifteen years as my personal assistant. But when I left AMJ after the debacle with Bruce Bowser, Kim was ready for a change.

She was flattered and perhaps slightly surprised that I viewed her as a potential partner in Premiere Executive Suites. But my offer was in line with how I've always operated: I don't care if you lack a glowing resume or multiple university degrees. It's about drive and personality.

Kim and her husband, Chris, made the leap to invest with me in Premiere Executive Suites, putting up $8,000 for 10 percent of the Toronto company. They were joined by Lois Roque, a veteran of the accommodations industry, who put in $10,000. Lois and Kim were both originally from Brampton but had never met. They clicked immediately. In 2003, their first year in operation, they posted a profit of about $10,000 in just six months. The following year they generated $1 million in sales and $120,000 in profit. They complemented each other well in growing the business and increased their combined stake in the company to 50 percent. Kim's husband also joined the company, doing maintenance, unit setup, and customer service, making it a true family venture.

Lois and Kim managed the Toronto business—which peaked with around 175 units and $10 million in revenue before selling—by not growing beyond their means or skill sets. For example, they regularly recorded light profits during the slower winter months and maintained 95 percent occupancy during the busy summer travel period. Over the years, Kim repeated a mantra: it's not the number of units you have that matters—it's your occupancy rate.

By early 2005, Premiere Executive Suites owned approximately $30 million in real estate and was generating $12 million in annual revenue. We had 450 suites in seven markets: St. John's, Halifax, Chester, Moncton (where we'd built a twenty-four–unit building at a cost of $3 million), Montréal, Toronto, and Calgary. Apart from Moncton, which was a franchise, each location was a joint venture between me and an operating partner.

Out West, I found a trusted partner in former Olympian Diane Jones-Konihowski. She was a member of Canada's national track and field team from 1967 to 1984, competing in the pentathlon, a gruelling combination of five events: hurdles, shot put, high jump, long jump, and an 800-metre run. I'd befriended her through AMJ Campbell's sponsorship of the Canadian Olympic team in Lillehammer, Norway, during the 1994 Winter Olympics, where she was part of the Canadian mission staff—the team sent to aid our Olympians. In the late 1990s, Diane served as a liaison between AMJ Campbell and the Canadian Olympic team, helping to secure athletes to appear at our corporate events, among them rower Silken Laumann and speed skaters Jeremy Wotherspoon and Catriona Le May Doan.

One year, as a surprise for my birthday, Diane took me to Olympic Park in Calgary and gave me the unique and most terrifying gift I've ever received: a bobsled ride. She still laughs when recalling the terrified look on my face as I strapped on a helmet and sat behind the Olympic driver. Diane knew that it would pain me to not be in control of the situation. I was dressed in a suit, and it was -25°C as we shot down the icy track at 120 kilometres per hour. And it was a gift that kept on giving because my neck hurt for a week after!

I saw Diane as an obvious operating partner for our Premiere Executive Suites operation in Calgary, although it took a few attempts to grab her interest. I remember calling her one day as I was down on my knees, making a bed. I was trying to convince her to join as a partner. Despite the initial hesitation, she and her husband, John Konihowski, a former CFL player and Grey Cup winner, partnered with me in the Calgary operations, initially mortgaging eight riverside condos at roughly $200,000 apiece. That quickly grew to fifty-two units, either owned or leased, in the upscale Eau Claire district.

When interviewed by the *Calgary Herald* in May 2003 and asked why a storied athlete like her would leave the sports world for the accommodation business, something she knew nothing about, she recalled that phone conversation and said that she was talking to me one day and happened to ask what I was doing. "That's when I figured if Tim Moore could make beds, I guess I can join the suites business," she explained. "I've cleaned units. I've shopped for inventory. Answering the phone, making the sale. You just roll up your sleeves and you do it. It's about learning the business from the ground up," she said.

The Calgary suites market was far more competitive than, say, Halifax. "We've got a ton of competition in this city," she acknowledged to the *Herald*. "But you know what? That's OK, I'm an athlete, I'm not afraid of competition."

A key driver to the success of Calgary's Premiere Suites was Dave Blackman, formerly of Cara Operations, who joined Diane and John in expanding to nearly two hundred units across thirty buildings.

There were also many market challenges to contend with during the early 2000s. For instance, it was very difficult to find cleaning staff in Alberta's hot labour market, and SARS scared many American tourists away from Canada. And yet Diane's team maintained an occupancy rate above 90 percent.

It's a hectic business, one in which you are always on call. If a unit floods, or a drunken tenant loses their key at 3:00 A.M., you must get out of bed and solve the problem. Perhaps not surprisingly, every time I saw Diane she told me I looked tired! "It can be a very stressful business. You'd see the ugly side of people, in addition to the good," Diane recalled. "I was glad we did it. But it was a tough business. It was a good seven years for us in the suites business. We did well and moved on to other things."

As in all my businesses, quality service was the key to beating the competition. I was relentless in upholding a reputation for integrity and excellence in meeting my customers' needs.

At its peak, Premiere Executive Suites was (and remains) the largest extended-stay accommodations provider in Canada, with 1,200 units. About 150 of those units were in the Halifax area, including more than a dozen units in the Bishop's Landing complex on the Halifax waterfront. In fact, those were among our very first units, and we leased them from Southwest Properties, the real estate company owned by developer Jim Spatz. That initial connection led to Southwest joining Premiere as a minority shareholder in the summer of 2002. "As that relationship grew bigger, it became obvious to both us and them that there were significant synergies," Spatz told Halifax's *Chronicle Herald* in an article that ran under the headline, "Spatz Checks into Premiere." "We own a lot of apartments in the Halifax region and those guys rent a lot of suites in the Halifax region," Spatz added. "This is what we hope will be a long-term relationship." I told the *Herald* there was "ideal chemistry" between the two companies.

Fast forward to 2010, and I was—once again—worn out by the travel required to manage a national, multi-province business. During a chat with Jim, we mutually agreed that it made sense for Southwest, which was in acquisition mode, to buy my majority stake in Premiere.

Southwest eventually bought out all my regional partners in the business: Diane Jones-Konihowski in Calgary, and Lois Roque and Kim Boydell in Toronto. Kim and Lois had diligently built Premiere's Toronto operation to 150 units and were netting $1 million in profit each year from $10 million in revenue. (My companies have always been heavily populated by female managers and executives, and Premiere was no exception; at one point, all our eighteen offices were owned and operated by talented women.)

For Kim and her husband, Chris, selling their stake in Premiere to Southwest Properties was life altering. "Partnering with Tim in the extended-stay accommodations business was perhaps the riskiest decision of my life, but it was also one of the best moves we ever made," she recalled, "one that ultimately gave us the financial freedom to retire early. And we have Tim to thank for a lot of our good fortune."

Like AMJ Campbell, Premiere Executive Suites did not start with a grand plan for national expansion. That wasn't the intent for either business, yet in both cases it was the outcome. I'm very growth-oriented, so long as that growth is sustainable and connected to a winning culture. Another reason is that I've never opened an office or branch without first securing a strong owner-operator—somebody who could be my partner on the ground, a person I trusted and with whom I had a good connection.

I built two highly respected national businesses using that formula. The right people in the right place became as valuable as well-located property. They appreciate in value as they gain experience and your working relationship deepens. You can build on their loyalty and individual drive. In short, the right partners on the ground are as foundational as bricks and mortar.

Chapter 9

Never Say Never

Surround yourself with people that are smarter than you, give them everything they need to grow, and your business will thrive.

RICHARD BRANSON

I COULD HAVE BEEN A DRAGON ON CBC'S POPULAR *Dragons' Den* program. Arlene Dickinson, noted Dragon, entrepreneur, marketer, and author, met me several years ago and suggested that, with my business background, I'd be a good member of the panel who assess pitches from business people wanting venture capital. I was flattered and went to the CBC studios in Toronto for an audition. But I was nervous as hell! I didn't make the cut. Certainly, I've had my share of people pitching me on business ideas over the years. Hundreds, in fact. People calling me, writing to me. Wanting money. I would always listen to the pitch. I have a busy mind; a little bit of undiagnosed ADHD? Maybe. I am adept at multi-tasking. I can have ten to fifteen things on the go at the same time. And I'm curious, always looking at the world for opportunities.

Many of the ventures I got involved with had a real estate component and were service oriented. And then, if I was going to have skin in the game, I insisted on having control with majority shares. Some pitches were crazy. Some I didn't have the energy for. And some weren't in my wheelhouse.

But I didn't let that stop me if I thought the opportunity was worthwhile. My venture into financial services is an example. Remember, I dropped math at the end of grade 10. Who would have thought that I would invest in a business sector that involved my greatest weakness? Of course, I had improved my financial literacy over the years. Business matters dictated that. I knew my way around financial statements. Still, financial services is not a business I would have pursued on my own.

I got into this line of work because one day I was chatting with Don MacVicar Sr., a very dear friend whom I'd known for over fifteen years. He was a former vice-president of the Bank of Nova Scotia. My son Chris was about to graduate in finance from Saint Mary's University at the time. Don's sons, Don Jr. and David, were working at a bank as mortgage brokers. This was a field Chris was interested in as well. I suggested that we should consider starting a mortgage lending business along with my son and his two sons.

Don agreed, so in 2008, we launched Premiere Mortgage Centre with all of us as partners. The company aimed to provide clients with the lowest possible mortgage rates, shopped from a variety of banks, for residential home purchases.

We named it Premiere Mortgage Centre to build on the Premiere branding we had with other ventures. It had started with Premiere Van Lines, then Premiere Executive Suites, Premiere Self Storage, Premiere Car Wash (a venture I started in 2006, eventually having three locations, all of which we sold within ten years), and now Premiere Mortgage Centre. We were building a reputation for excellent customer service across various businesses.

Chris joined when he graduated, and together with Don's sons, they worked hard to develop the business.

Around the same time, independently of Premiere Mortgage Centre, I was introduced to the idea of alternative lending. This is a situation where a client needs money faster often than a bank can offer, or when the banks are reluctant to lend for a variety of reasons. John Chandler, a good friend and lawyer in Chester who handles a lot of real estate transactions, approached me with an offer to loan money to someone—short-term—for the purchase of a piece of property. It was an appealing proposal. John and I would charge a 4 percent fee and 12 percent interest. The loan amount was for roughly 60 percent of the property value. Even if the borrower defaulted on the loan (which was unlikely) we could sell the property to recoup our money. I couldn't see any real downside. I was intrigued, so I agreed. And it worked out well. We made good money on this one-off deal.

All the way along, I was speaking to Chris about it. I trusted his judgment and expertise in financial matters. He thought it was a good opportunity as well. Through John, we were subsequently introduced to Phil Noble, who had been in the alternative lending business for years. From London, Ontario, Phil is a brilliant financial guy with an incredible mind for business and highly principled. At that time, he had a small office in Halifax, where he was trying to drum up business while commuting back and forth from London. With few connections in Halifax, he was having trouble raising the necessary money for loans. We joined forces, and together we did a few deals that also had excellent outcomes. While we made these loan arrangements, he let us pick his brain, teaching us an incredible amount about the industry.

Chris and I became even more intrigued by this alternative sector of the lending industry. We owned real estate. I knew it to be a valuable asset. Now, we could loan money in real estate. There was little risk.

Meanwhile, Premiere Mortgage was limping along in its start-up phase. I was betting that the new company could do $50 million to $100 million in mortgages in the first year. But that didn't happen. We couldn't make good headway. We had terrific people. Extensive contacts. High revenue. Great concept. But the profit margins were tight.

Chris and I were antsy—and we had this other financial side hustle going on, which was yielding better returns. I couldn't see the light at the end of the tunnel for really good profits with the Premiere Mortgage venture. In hindsight, that impatience was wrong-footed. Premiere Mortgage Centre went on to become one of the top five mortgage broker businesses in Canada. We could have kept our equity in that business.

Instead, we decided to start an alternative money lending business called Atlantic Signature Mortgage & Loan. Friends and family were surprised. "Not another business!" several said. But Chris and I were confident and ambitious for this new venture.

I launched Atlantic Signature with roughly $1 million of our own capital and with an equal amount borrowed from our bank. At that time, the alternative lending industry was often viewed as a questionable enterprise, which wasn't unjustified. I'd heard a few horror stories. You could be seen as a loan shark—tough guys taking advantage of people who are in a tight spot and unable to secure mortgages or loans with banks. If clients are late by one day in repaying their loans, some companies can be ruthless and seize assets almost immediately. We were very cognizant of this risk to our reputation as business leaders. From the outset, we wanted to clearly differentiate ourselves from the other short-term lenders, some of which were simply one-person, fly-by-night operations. We wanted to be more empathetic as lenders, extending our brand of above-expectation customer service.

In less than a year, Chris and I had placed the entire $2 million. By the end of that first year, we'd pocketed a profit of $100,000. This was a good investment. Our intuition had been right. We just needed more money to increase our book of business.

The local alternative lending market had many formal and private players. Among those private lenders were brothers Keith and David Dexter. Keith and David are best known in the Halifax business community for their twenty years in the car business (they sold their Audi and Subaru dealerships to Rob Steele in 2008). But they've been involved in upwards of thirty businesses across a variety of sectors, including insurance, self-storage, and mergers and acquisitions. Their model is simple: buy it, build it, sell it. Keith and Dave are professional, talented, and each possess exceptional personalities and skill sets.

Around 2005, a few years before selling their car business, the brothers started dabbling in the lending business. Like me, they hadn't planned to loan money. They started only after being approached for short-term financial help by partners, friends, and associates in their network.

Eventually, they noticed that they were being approached by potential clients who had also reached out to us at Atlantic Signature. Keith and I had never met, but he realized that we were all mulling over many of the same deals. The tipping point came when he noticed that we were both considering a loan for a beautiful property in Mahone Bay on the South Shore of Nova Scotia.

Keith tracked down my number and called me out of the blue while I was on vacation in Barbados. He's the type of businessman who won't hesitate to pick up the phone and get a conversation going with a competitor if he believes there's potential synergy. I admired that.

"Tim, we're butting heads out there on some good files," he told me. "We should talk. What are *you* doing? What are *we* doing? Maybe there's an opportunity to work together."

I agreed, so we arranged to meet in Chester. Although we were more formerly established, it didn't require much convincing to see that it made sense to combine our book of business with the Dexters' portfolio of loans. Within a few months, we'd joined as partners in Atlantic Signature Mortgage & Loan, with Chris and I holding 55 percent of the shares.

We set up a physical office in Halifax, hired more staff, and—most importantly—assembled an advisory board made up of top local business figures, including Rob Steele, who owned about forty car dealerships; Fred Smithers, founder of Secunda Marine Services; Paul Goodman, chartered accountant and partner in BDO Canada LLP; Jeff Somerville, formerly senior vice-president of TD Bank; and Scott McCrea, CEO of the Armour Group, a leading real estate entity.

Those efforts, especially our blue-chip advisory board, gave us a level of professionalism that was missing from many of our competitors. It projected discipline, structure, and confidence. As a result, we quickly became the go-to direct lending organization in Atlantic Canada. People trusted us—so much so that we were RBC's alternative lender for the region, meaning the bank funnelled business to us that it couldn't pursue, but which it knew would be a good fit for a more flexible lender like us. We would never have secured that trust from RBC if not for the structure and professionalism we implemented.

Great partnerships have a certain magic of combined talents. Keith and I are similar in many ways. We're always eyeing the next project, the next business, the next opportunity. Which means we're sometimes viewed as "eccentric" or "crazy" because of our constant deal-making and brainstorming. We've both been described as the Tasmanian Devil, the Looney Tunes character, because of our frenetic energy. We're both "big picture" investors who excel at business development, with little patience for day-to-day operations.

As Keith liked to explain, he is the guy who throws shit at the wall. David is the one who figures out how to make it work. In my case, Chris handled the operational side of our lending business in a methodical, calm, and highly efficient manner. He was superb at assessing loan opportunities. I was the wild brainstormer. We would often hold meetings in which Keith and I would spin a whirlwind of ideas. "What just happened? What do they want to do *now*?" David and Chris would remark, slightly shell-shocked, as the meeting ended. But they were instrumental in being the voices of reason and measured thinking, which kept us focussed and on track. We eventually made David the company president with Chris as vice-president.

Our goal was to be the biggest and the best alternative lender on the East Coast. Contrary to what some people assumed, our lending business did not involve so-called "distressed lending." We were not acting as a lender of last resort for people on the verge of bankruptcy. Instead, we were often providing "bridge financing" for projects that the big banks either wouldn't loan money for or took too long approving.

Consider the example of an entrepreneur who wants to construct a commercial building on a piece of land. Banks can be reluctant to loan money for such projects so the developer needs a loan to get started. Once they have a physical building to use as collateral, a bank will likely step in with financing. In other words, we provided loans to "bridge" entrepreneurs to more traditional lending.

Our loans were always short-term, backed by real estate, and carried interest of roughly 12 percent, plus fees. We also loaned money for residential home purchases, but for no more than 75 percent of the total home cost. That ensured that there was equity in the property in case we had to foreclose and sell the asset. But that rarely happened because we were selective of the people and projects we chose to back.

As private lenders, we offered flexibility that the big banks often lack. For example, we had one wealthy American client who borrowed money from us to buy West Ironbound, a sheep-populated island along the South Shore. But then the 2008 financial crisis hit and that client—who had been worth around $40 million—found himself in a compromised financial position. For two years, he didn't make a single payment against the West Ironbound loan. We didn't panic, and we didn't pull the loan. The client stayed in regular communication with us. We knew that as soon as his position improved he'd make good on the loan, which he did.

As an amusing aside, we were asked to remove the sheep before the deal closed.

"Chris," I asked my son, "do you want to get a boat and pick up the sheep?"

"Huh? I don't have a 'sheep' boat."

"You could rent a boat."

"A boat for a herd of sheep?"

It was like a Monty Python sketch.

In the end, I abdicated responsibility for the sheep. The other side took care of the situation—relocating the herd elsewhere—and the deal closed.

You run into odd situations in business, which give you a treasure trove of stories.

Atlantic Signature was a great business. At one point, we planned on expansion into Ontario and the United States but eventually concluded that the work and risk involved in those markets (which we didn't know as well) weren't worth the returns. We understood the Atlantic Canadian mentality and clientele because we lived here. Which made it much easier to gauge risk.

I respected and always carefully considered Chris's and David's opinions on every matter. They were the ones running the business. On one occasion, a financing deal came up in Chester. I thought it looked promising. There was a lot of equity in the property.

But after Chris analyzed the opportunity, he said, "Dad, we're not going to finance it."

In a kidding manner, I said, "Wait a minute. How many shares do I have in Atlantic Mortgage & Loan? How many shares do you have? Because I think I have more than you." I was jerking his chain by suggesting I could pull rank to make the decision I wanted.

Chris and I are close—and in some ways, different in personalities. But I completely trusted his assessments of loan pitches.

"No, Dad. We're not going to do the deal," he reiterated before calmly explaining his reasoning.

I accepted his decision. It's important not to think you're always more knowledgeable or right. You don't know everything. Together, the four of us were an ideal mix of vision, ambition, discipline, and caution. We'd grown the mortgage and loan business to a size we could manage well. We'd placed hundreds of millions of dollars in loans. And in twelve years of business, we had only been forced to pull loans on six properties. As Keith said at the time, we had Atlantic Signature "hitting on all cylinders."

It was time to sell to a bigger player in the field. I had other ventures in the works, and the Dexters had bought an insurance business they wanted to grow, so it was the right time for all of us to move on.

As is often the case, we had a potential buyer targeted from the start: Credit Union Atlantic (CUA). The four of us agreed on a figure we'd like to sell it for. Keith was delegated the task of pursuing a deal with CUA. David and Chris were responsible for the due diligence.

Within a matter of weeks, we'd agreed to terms and the deal closed about six months later, in 2020. (CUA has since purchased other lending companies, further expanding their book of business.) Chris owned 22 percent of Atlantic Signature, and with the sale he was able to pay off the mortgage on his home. As a young man, he had done well.

The key takeaway from my adventures in the lending business is that you should never say never to opportunities you might have thought were beyond your scope. Start small. Start cautiously. Get a feel for it. Be involved. Learn the details, the ins and outs, the risks, the boundaries. Then if you feel ready to go bigger, find partners who have the skills you lack. Having that brain trust can make all the difference between a fiasco and huge success. Because no entrepreneur has the complete package of skills and knowledge, not even one with decades of experience and several businesses under his belt, including trying to solve the problem of an abandoned sheep herd on a remote island.

As of this writing, Chris and I have started a new lending company, Maritime Edge Mortgage & Loan. Some things never change. I couldn't help myself. In the first two months, the company is oversubscribed, and we're financing over $3 million in business already.

Like I said, never say never—again!

Chapter 10

Avoiding the Pitfalls of a Family Business

Working with family demands patience, compromise, and a deep understanding that the business is part of a greater legacy.

MARTIN LOPEZ
Chair at ABS-CBN Corporation
and Vice-chair at Lopez Holdings Corporation

RIGHT FROM THE BEGINNING, BERNARDINE AND I AGREED on how to raise our two boys, Matthew and Chris, who are two years apart. Love them. And discipline them. We didn't want to spoil them or encourage a sense of entitlement. Wealthy parents can often rob their children of ambition by giving them too much, too early. We laid out the ground rules. We will pay for education. But then you have to make your own way.

I had another rule. I didn't want them to be in the moving business.

I had built the most successful moving empire in Canada and had every opportunity to bring my boys into the business. On one occasion, Jason, one of my two sons from my first marriage, worked in our AMJ Campbell operations in Toronto and Calgary, but he soon returned to the United States, where his older brother and mother had made their lives.

If people could have witnessed the stressful life I led for twenty-five years, they would understand my decision. I sacrificed a lot of quality life with my family, with Bernardine, in my drive to make my business a success. Bernardine raised our boys often on her own. One year, she brought the boys to the airport dressed in their Hallowe'en costumes, so I could see how cute they looked. I was in transit to another destination and didn't have time to come home. The moving sector is tough, as I have said. I ground myself to a pulp a couple of times. I'm not feeling sorry for myself. I did it to myself. Willingly. I truly loved the business. Every major issue, every claim, every major hire—I was the one who executed it.

I told Bernardine: "I don't want that life for our boys."

But that didn't stop Matthew, my eldest with Bernardine, from starting a small moving operation when he finished university. If you consider all the stories of my career that I've described in this book, multiply that number tenfold to account for the tales my boys heard around the dinner table. They learned first-hand about the joys, grit, and missteps of entrepreneurship, which fuelled their own ambition. In his early twenties, Matthew bought a pickup truck and spent hours—days!—out on the street plastering advertisements on public utility posts across downtown Halifax. Just like I had done in my youth. His work ethic was amazing. He took loads to Toronto, and eventually, he handled a move to Boston—an opportunity to outperform me and my disastrous, money-losing misadventure to move a client in the early stages of my career. And Matthew was quick to point out his one-upmanship!

"My Dad took a load to Boston in his first few weeks of business for $75 plus gas," he would regale others. "He lost money on it. I did a trip and made a nice profit!"

There's nothing like being an example to your children—of what not to do!

He was gutsy and determined—hmmm, like me! He soon bought a thirty-foot truck and drove to New York to move a friend of mine, lawyer Larry Pringle. I'm not sure Matthew had a licence to transport goods to New York. But he did it anyway, and it was two weeks after 9/11. We have a picture of him with his moving truck in New York surrounded by fire trucks and police cars. Nothing would stop him. I admire that greatly. It's how you need to think as an entrepreneur.

From the time our two boys were young, Bernardine and I had taught Matthew and Chris about determination and money. I was addressing my own childhood trauma in this regard. I wanted them to grow up with an appreciation for money; the importance of avoiding debt and living within their means; how to earn money, how to save it, and how to manage it. They had lemonade stands as children. They sold golf balls. They cut grass and did other landscaping jobs. They had all sorts of money-making gigs. I taught them about the stock market and gave them a few shares in CamVec, the parent of AMJ Campbell when it went public, so they could learn first-hand.

"Dad! Dad!" they would squeal, running to the front door upon my arrival home. "We lost money today! The shares dropped!" Or conversely, "Dad! Dad! We made five bucks today. The shares went up!" It's a great way to help children understand the market. There's nothing like watching the magic—and the possible disappointment—in real time!

Our younger son, Chris, as I detailed in the previous chapter, had a great interest and facility with money. I had always reinforced the fact that 95 percent of millionaires in Canada are seriously involved in real estate. I told both boys not to reinvent the wheel and to make sure to buy property.

Since the age of ten, Chris had been saving money made from summer jobs and odd chores. By the age of eighteen, he had saved $20,000, all invested in stocks. He witnessed my buying spree of condos at the start of Premiere Executive Suites, and he wanted to buy one. I didn't give him one. But I co-signed a loan for him after he put his twenty grand down as a deposit. He had to buy furniture for it and manage the upkeep.

Matthew, after his brief moving truck stint, cycled through a variety of career options. He is a voracious learner. He has a total of six post-secondary degrees, including three master's degrees, covering business and health sciences. He has five certifications and licences, as a chartered accountant, as a first aid responder, a real estate broker, an expert in Danish language, culture, and society, and in Swedish. Like many young people, he found it hard to chart his path at the beginning.

I will never forget my pride over a review that a head nurse recently gave him when he was placed in a nursing home for a month as part of his health-care training. That is not an easy job. And not a fun job by any means. It requires empathy, patience, and kindness. The head nurse reported that Matthew never stood around waiting to be told what to do. He did whatever was required without complaint or hesitation. That says a lot about his caring character.

After some time, he settled on real estate as one of his key interests. He was shrewd about identifying good properties. He scoured listings online. He checked out neighbourhoods. He worked alongside top realtors. "Dad, we should buy this place in Halifax," he would say to me, full of enthusiasm. Often, we did. He's a dreamer. His mind works like mine, bubbling with ideas.

He eventually owned several condos, with me co-signing loans after he came up with the deposit. He is also involved as a partner in several of our businesses and is especially good in sales.

In our family, real estate was a bit of a healthy addiction. Which is why, in the fall of 2011, we couldn't resist a beautiful and alluring property. Chris and his wife, Lizzie, had come with me to tour Oceanstone Inn and Cottages, a 7.5-acre waterfront property overlooking Indian Harbour on St. Margarets Bay, about forty-five minutes outside Halifax on the South Shore. Matthew was overseas at the time, studying.

I'd been alerted to the listing by a friend of mine, Tom McGuire, a real estate agent who lived nearby. Tom thought I might be interested in the property, which had charming waterside cottages, a restaurant called Rhubarb, a convention centre, a banquet hall, and a main office—all located less than five kilometres from the iconic village of Peggys Cove.

I didn't offer Chris and Lizzie any specifics about the property. I wanted them to arrive free of expectations. Worst case, we'd have a nice walk by the water if the opportunity didn't grab us.

Ah, but we were completely enchanted! The sun was out, the water sparkled, and the view across the bay was mesmerizing. We arrived during a wedding ceremony, which further added to the charm of the place—and hinted at the commercial value of the property.

I could feel the familiar ping-pinging of my brain as I silently began envisioning what could be.

Work would be involved. And money. Lots of it. That much was obvious. Despite its beauty and location, Oceanstone was losing money, and the owners—the MacInnis family—were struggling to pay for basic upkeep and improvements. The kitchen in the main lodge was dilapidated. The restaurant was also in disrepair. In fact, it had been closed for a couple of years due to low traffic and staffing issues. Roads around the resort were unpaved and dented with potholes.

Getting back into their car at the end of our tour, Chris looked at Lizzie.

"Oh, no," he said upon seeing his wife's dreamy expression.

"Oh, yes," Lizzie replied, smiling.

Off we set in our separate cars. Soon Chris and Lizzie, on speaker phone, called me on my cell. We spent the next half hour during the drive home discussing a potential purchase and how we could turn the resort around.

Bernardine and I had known Lizzie for many years through our friendship with her parents, Carol and Colin Dodds, who had a house in Chester. Colin was president of Saint Mary's University in Halifax for fifteen years and has maintained a relationship with the institution where he still teaches. Chris and Lizzie first met as teenagers during the summers. It wasn't until later, in their mid-twenties, that they reconnected, began dating, and eventually married. I'd always felt that Lizzie possessed many of the qualities essential to entrepreneurialism: smarts, drive, an outgoing personality, and an incredible work ethic. When she lived in Ottawa, during the first stint of her career, she worked as chief of staff for Peter Van Loan, a cabinet minister in Stephen Harper's government. She was the youngest chief of staff on Parliament Hill and was on call 24-7. I should point out that she was voted best chief of staff on Parliament Hill. That takes intelligence and superb organizational skills.

After she and Chris started dating, she often expressed interest in being a business owner. And I, ever the enthusiastic entrepreneur, began making suggestions, trying to convince her to partner with me in a venture or start her own.

More than once, I asked her, "When are you going to start your own business?"

One of my ideas was a company focussed on selling and cleaning winter floor mats—the special mats you dry your boots on during the winter months. Not surprisingly, Lizzie didn't bite on that riveting idea. The next idea: a company focussed on portable, cubic storage units. That went over like a lead balloon as well.

But Oceanstone, well, that grabbed her interest. She'd fallen for the place. She could see that the roofs needed fixing, the lawn needed re-sodding, and that the garden was overgrown, but those issues didn't outweigh her enthusiasm for the potential.

"This is it. This is my business. This is the entrepreneurial adventure," she recalls telling Chris. At the time of our Oceanstone viewing, she was working at the Halifax Port Authority in communications and public relations—a "normal job," as she has described it. Naturally, she had questions and reservations. Which we worked through. She and Chris both believed that together we could dramatically improve the physical and operational sides of the business.

I thought carefully about the possibility of working together as a family. Chris and I worked well together at Atlantic Signature Mortgage & Loan. There had been disagreements, but we always managed them well. In AMJ Campbell, my brothers had been involved as well as close friends. But immediate family is different. And my daughter-in-law's involvement was also important to consider. I wanted to make sure that business wouldn't interfere with our close family dynamic. This can happen. Money and power can hurt relationships. Just have a look at the Rogers family disputes. And the problems of the Phelan family, who were owners of Cara Foods that supplied meals for Swiss Chalet, Harvey's, and Air Canada as well as other airlines.

The key, I knew, was to avoid role confusion. Make it clear who is the ultimate decisionmaker. Moreover, the right mentality has to be in place. I trusted and admired Chris and Lizzie. I knew they were a good, hard-working team.

Lizzie knew that I move quickly in making decisions, so she wasn't surprised when we made a successful offer on the property—$2 million—and closed the deal on December 9, 2011, less than two months after our Thanksgiving weekend viewing. In fact, I was literally on the phone with a paving company as we were signing the purchase papers because we needed the roads within the resort paved before the first snowfall of the year.

Lizzie quit her PR job to be an entrepreneur. What would be our ten-year love affair with Oceanstone had begun. Originally, the property contained a single small house, which was used for Buddhist spiritual and yoga retreats. The owners later added several cabins. At the time of our purchase, it consisted of five waterfront cottages (the largest of which was a three-bedroom captain's house), each with a deck overlooking the water and a fire pit out front. Additionally, there was a mix of suites, guestrooms, and cottages both in and near the main lodge, for a total of twenty units.

During the winter and spring of 2012, we started a massive renovation of the entire resort. We added a new office and lobby, laid more than an acre of sod (against the advice of our landscaper, who said it was too early in the season), upgraded all the cottages, and laid paver stones throughout the property. We had a wedding booked on-site for the May long weekend, which meant that we had a hard deadline to complete our planned overhaul.

It was a true team and family effort because the original ownership group consisted of myself and Bernardine, Chris and Lizzie, Matthew, and Lizzie's parents, Colin and Carol. Each of us helped get the resort shipshape for that first wedding of the season, which we knew would impact future success. It had to go well. Even Lizzie's parents helped in the cleanup.

Our planned kitchen upgrades weren't yet complete, so the six-course Italian meal had to be prepared in one of the units (with the food inspector's blessing, of course), and Chris served as our stand-in bartender. We pulled it all together in time, though barely!

We were often praised for improving and modernizing Oceanstone, while also maintaining what had always made it special (and what we had all felt while first touring the property): the resort's enticing atmosphere of peace and calmness. Again and again, we heard long-time guests make comments to the effect of, "You kept the essence of Oceanstone while taking it to the next level," or "You increased the comfort without sacrificing the spirit." We greatly appreciated those comments and took each one as a testament to the care, effort, and money we'd poured into the resort.

By 2016, we employed fifty people, and the resort was thriving. Our wedding schedule was fully booked through 2017, and we were hosting corporate events every week. We were considering an additional $750,000 in improvements, for a pool, gym, hot tub, and ten new rooms.

As with any business upgrade, our restoration efforts came up against many challenges, including the presence of an on-site restaurant. The restaurant industry is notoriously difficult to succeed in, with few truly profitable examples among the many, many failures. From my perspective, restaurant ownership was the riskiest element of the whole Oceanstone venture. Rhubarb needed a reboot and refresh. We renovated the entire restaurant and converted the top floor of the building into five additional units, taking us up to ten more units, to a total of thirty.

During our first season, we hired a chef and ran Rhubarb ourselves. But I soon sensed an opportunity after being introduced to a young couple, Jim and Diane Buckle. Diane was a part-time teacher; Jim was a sous-chef at a restaurant in Peggys Cove. They shared a dream of owning their own restaurant, so I suggested that they run Rhubarb. It would be their restaurant, to be operated as they saw fit. Our cut would be 8 percent of sales. Initially, Diane—who had a perfect personality for front-of-house hospitality—passed on that offer, unsure if she and Jim should make the leap to restaurant ownership. But over the course of three meetings, they warmed to the idea, signed on, and found immediate success as owners. The restaurant won numerous awards.

Another hurdle—one faced by many entrepreneurs in Nova Scotia—was the province's excessive and stifling red tape. In 2016, the Halifax Regional Municipality took us to court for allegedly exceeding the scope of a building permit we'd received for Oceanstone in 2012. Specifically, the municipality took issue with some very minor improvements we made to our main building: insulation to prevent heat loss, and the addition of a conference room and two offices—changes which covered one thousand square feet, a fraction of the building's overall square footage. All I did was finish the second floor of the building. Not a big deal.

I don't consider myself to be an antagonistic or litigious person, but in this case, I was infuriated by what I saw as crushing regulations against growth, enforced to meet the letter of the law, not its spirit. Plus, we were located forty-five minutes from the downtown core. What did they care about some relatively minor renovations on a rural property?

Disgusted, I told *The Chronicle Herald* that I was suspending any further development at Oceanstone until the situation was resolved. Why waste our time or financial resources? My businesses have thrived in part because of continued investment. You must always be putting money back into your ventures. But Nova Scotia's regulations deter investment, limiting economic growth and job creation.

The resulting article ran on the front page of the *Herald* business section on October 22, 2016, under the headline, "Oceanstone's Moore Fed Up with N.S."

"A serial entrepreneur is threatening to stop investing in his Oceanstone Seaside Resort in Indian Harbour—and maybe even start selling off his other Nova Scotia business assets—out of growing frustration with what he calls senseless red tape," read the article's lead sentence. I was quoted, saying that I thought the regulations were absolute nuts—no holding back on my anger!—and that I might as well pull out of Nova Scotia.

Causing a stir in the media is a good thing!

Jordi Morgan, then the Atlantic region vice-president for the Canadian Federation of Independent Business, backed me up, telling the *Herald*: "I wouldn't blame [Tim] if he packed up and left. And some people have.... [Some] inspectors are trying to apply regulations to the letter of the law without any consideration of the policy objectives. It's counter-productive.... They don't seem to take into consideration what the benefit is to the general community."

To remedy our situation, the municipality suggested we could either seek a development agreement or apply to subdivide our land. I couldn't believe it—all for a few hundred square feet of extra space on an eight-acre property. It was ridiculous. Fortunately, with the help of a lawyer friend, we resolved the situation without costs and only some minor inconvenience. We continued to put resources into Oceanstone. And I did not divest my Nova Scotia holdings.

My working relationship with Lizzie, who had the lead role as president of Oceanstone, was terrific, even though we are very different in approach and temperament. Like Chris, who was busy running Atlantic Signature Mortgage & Loan, she is more practical and methodical than I am. She is more likely to create a detailed plan with specific steps for achieving her desired goal, whereas I'm more impulsive if I judge something to be a good idea.

Once again, as with previous partnerships, our combined differences made for a successful blending of skills. And I was careful to develop our business relationship in a thoughtful manner. Early on, I sensed that it was awkward for Chris and Lizzie to transition between family and business topics at the Sunday dinner table, which was part of our ritual, often involving her parents as well. Understandably, it was initially difficult for Lizzie to have a debate on some aspect of Oceanstone's operations, and then sit down to dinner and discuss the weather. With time, however, it became easier to balance those two sides of our relationship. And I always stressed to Chris and Lizzie that the family connection was paramount, the business second.

Which is not to say that our Oceanstone adventure was free of disagreements. For example, there was an ongoing debate about whether we should install a swimming pool. I wanted one as I thought it would add to the appeal of the property. Lizzie and Chris disagreed. I was close to overruling them but in the end backed down. After all, there was the sea! And Lizzie and Chris still laugh when recalling the day that a large order of Pottery Barn furniture arrived at the resort, which I'd ordered in Toronto without consulting Lizzie.

She could only shake her head. "How much did this cost?" she asked at the time.

We always smoothed over the bumps in our business collaboration. I was very confident in Lizzie's leadership.

She is a master marketer. And that's exactly what we needed to promote Oceanstone, which, considering its proximity to Halifax, wasn't well known when we bought it. As newlyweds, Chris and Lizzie had many friends who were also organizing weddings. But few had heard of Oceanstone. There was obvious potential to make it a wedding destination, if we implemented the necessary upgrades. For instance, the main hall had a dilapidated bathroom, yet it had been used to host weddings with 150 people. That had to change.

Lizzie could easily relate to the stress of weddings, and she addressed all the typical concerns. We provided full one-stop service, for example. We handled everything. That made it especially easy for out-of-town couples to book their special event in Nova Scotia.

Although each wedding was unique in its own way, most followed a similar format. A rehearsal dinner usually took place on the Friday, either a barbecue or a lobster supper, which would allow everyone to meet, settle in, and get comfortable. Saturday would start with a breakfast with options for excursions during the day. The ceremony would usually take place by the water in the late afternoon with the stunning view in the background. Then it was off to the celebration dinner, held in the Great Room in the main lodge, followed by a dance on the lower level, overlooking the gardens.

We debated how to manage the wedding business. One issue involved how many weddings we could host at one time. I asked Lizzie why we didn't book multiple weddings per weekend. But Lizzie argued that hosting more than one wedding at once would diminish the intimacy. She believed in one wedding per weekend. All the wedding party and their closest guests would stay at the resort for the weekend. There wouldn't be anyone staying at the resort who wasn't connected to the client's wedding. They had Oceanstone to themselves. That meant that if someone saw an unfamiliar face at the resort, they'd feel comfortable saying hello, knowing that this person was also affiliated with the wedding, perhaps an uncle or cousin they hadn't yet met.

I saw a chance to boost revenue, but Lizzie realized that extra revenue would come at the expense of our offering, the quality of which quickly spread through word-of-mouth referrals. I didn't view the issue from the perspective of a bride and groom, who preferred exclusivity. Lizzie astutely viewed the situation from the customers' perspective.

And she had a solution. She boosted our total number of weddings by creatively offering mid-week ceremonies, an idea new to the local market. For many couples and their families, a wedding required taking a full week off work, to allow for travel and setup. If your family was taking a week off to fly to Halifax for your wedding, it didn't matter if the ceremony was held on a Saturday or a Wednesday or a Thursday. Some couples even preferred having weekday weddings because it meant they could book the top photographers, whose weekend schedules were booked months and even years in advance.

As wedding planner, Lizzie would spend her time whirling around the resort, ensuring everything went to plan—or as close to plan as possible! Our schedule was so busy that we couldn't fit all the requests into our summer calendar. We also consistently won Gold and Silver among wedding venues in *The Coast* newspaper's annual Best of Halifax Awards.

Lizzie took Oceanstone from an unknown treasure to a nationally known resort. After three or four years in the business, I couldn't travel anywhere without someone asking me about Oceanstone. The highlight of that work was having Oceanstone mentioned in *Elle* Canada, a national fashion and lifestyle magazine. The summer was obviously our peak season, but Lizzie also kept our winter bookings up with music nights (featuring musicians like Lennie Gallant and Laura Smith) and women's retreats, including two or three hosted by my friend and Canadian fashion icon Jeanne Beker (who also joined as a minority owner of Oceanstone).

Over our ten years of ownership, we saw countless people arrive—particularly to corporate retreats—frazzled and burnt out. They'd inevitably put their phones away (or at least pick them up less often), sit by the water, and almost be forced to disconnect from their hectic lives and stuffed schedules. They had time to breathe. By the end of a two- or three-day stay, they'd leave noticeably less stressed.

Those events, combined with the host of tourism awards we won (including the Tourism Industry Association of Nova Scotia's Best Business Award in 2018) helped us stay open year-round, whereas the previous owners had closed during the low-traffic winter months. We felt it was important for the community to have Oceanstone open year-round as an economic generator and employer.

For years, Lizzie liked to joke that Oceanstone was her first baby. And then she and Chris had some human babies—a son and a daughter, William and Victoria. This changing lifestyle factor contributed to our reluctant decision to sell the property in 2021. Before they had children, it was no problem for Lizzie to work a wedding until 3:00 A.M. and then get up at 7:00 A.M. to oversee breakfast service. Once they became parents, they maintained a delicate balancing act of daycare drop-offs and babysitters for a couple of years, but Lizzie gradually reduced her involvement in the day-to-day operations. We hired a full-time general manager in 2015.

All of us were sentimental about Oceanstone. We had a deep emotional attachment to this magical place. But there were business realities we also took into consideration in deciding to sell. After a decade as owners, we were clearing about $200,000 a year in profit from the business, but it was a seven-days-a-week concern. Annual profit of $200,000 wasn't worth the time and mental energy that we committed to the resort each year, especially since we had other businesses to focus on.

We sold to Dean Leland, a seasoned restaurateur and business executive, who'd entered as a managing partner a few years earlier. Dean, who'd previously been a fifty-fifty partner in the highly successful Bicycle Thief restaurant in Halifax, was eager to increase his stake in Oceanstone. We feel blessed knowing the business has continued to flourish under his leadership. And Rhubarb maintained its high standard and award-winning ways with Jim and Diane remaining on as operators for several years after the sale. It was named Taste of Nova Scotia's Restaurant of the Year in 2022.

In 2019, I was honoured at the annual Peter Wilson Dinner, hosted by the Family Business Association Atlantic to celebrate the leadership of a top local family business. Lizzie made a speech about our partnership at Oceanstone. "We balanced each other out," she said of our professional collaboration. "Tim has taught me over the years how to look at things in a different way—to embrace change and new opportunities and to look at the positives in everything.... Not everybody can work with their father-in-law. I've been very, very lucky to be able to do it. And I really appreciated him mentoring me through the different phases.... To be given the opportunity to grow and find my passion with Oceanstone was amazing and I want to thank Tim," she continued, addressing me directly. "Your passion and your knowledge are one of a kind, truly incredible."

I was moved to tears.

For me, it was immensely satisfying to see someone—especially a family member—find their footing as an entrepreneur. I never would have succeeded in any of my businesses without people like Lizzie. And it's all the sweeter that she's family. How blessed am I to have a daughter-in-law whom I love dearly.

Our family affair with real estate was not over—and still isn't. In 2009, when the deal to sell Premiere Suites to Southwest Properties happened, I had to abide by a standard non-compete clause, which meant I'd have to wait at least five years before starting another suites business, if that was something I wanted to pursue.

Initially it wasn't.

We had bought Oceanstone resort the year after we sold Premiere Executive Suites. That wasn't a suites business, and it scratched my itch for more real estate.

But then Chris and Matthew, ever keen about real estate, approached me with a plan to start a small suites provider.

"Come on, Dad, what can we do together?" they asked.

"I'm trying to retire," I replied in a good-natured manner. "You guys won't let me," I laughed.

I admire my boys. They understand the value of hard work and the need to make sacrifices. Their enthusiasm reignited my own.

I told them that my second suites venture would have to be modest. We'd dabble. Buy more real estate. Build a profitable business. But we would not pursue growth beyond Nova Scotia.

That was the beginning of Moore Suites, which we launched in 2014. My sons partnered with me as major shareholder. If they wanted more shares, they would have to come up with more money. I emphasized that they needed to respect one another. I wouldn't be around forever, I reminded them, and it was important that they look after each other with fairness and respect.

In all honesty, I had to help them navigate their relationship as brothers in business. That meant being frank with them about their skills and abilities and where they would best be put to use. One issue that arose was that the boys worked best in different capacities, not as co-managers. They're different from one another, as all siblings are. It was settled that Matthew would work in sales, while Chris took more of a leadership and management position.

We adopted the same approach as we had for Premiere Executive Suites. Stellar customer service. Utmost professionalism. Staff in neat uniforms who greeted each customer upon arrival. Quality furniture and linens. We installed 52-inch flat screen TVs, in-suite washer-dryers, fully equipped kitchens. In many of our units, we supplied Nespresso machines and Bose sound systems. Wi-Fi was free. A staff member was on call 24-7 to help with any issue.

Unfortunately, one unintended consequence of starting Moore Suites was the dissolution of my decades-long friendship with Suzanne Bachur. Together we'd worked to grow Premiere Suites from nothing to 1,200 units. After selling my shares, Suzanne stayed with Southwest Properties to help manage their Premiere units. My decision to start Moore Suites and thus compete against Southwest hurt Suzanne, who saw it as a betrayal of our friendship. I still feel badly about the fracturing of our relationship because Premiere Executive Suites would not have been as successful without her commitment, personality, incredible work ethic, and financial savvy.

But what few people knew, including Suzanne, was that Moore Suites was struggling at the beginning. In fact, for about five years we could barely draw a profit from the business, no matter our effort. To help get us started, I had purchased $1 million worth of furniture for our first forty to fifty units, with $750,000 of that cost being financed over five years. That dragged us down a bit. We were actually losing money for the first years.

The biggest problem was the advent of Airbnb, the online marketplace for short- and long-term accommodations, which started operating in Canada around 2009. It took time for it to catch on. But once it did, the shared-economy accommodation model completely upended the market. With Premiere Executive Suites, we'd had four competitors. Now, suddenly, we had thousands of competitors. Anyone with a spare attic, basement, or granny suite could enter the hospitality business. Needless to say, our timing for re-entering the market was problematic.

I start a business for one primary reason: to make money. Those money-losing years in the suites business—a business I knew better than anyone in Atlantic Canada—were tough. Chris was equally disenchanted with the company's performance.

"Why are we in this business, Dad?" he asked me one day. We were still involved with Atlantic Signature Mortgage & Loan and Oceanstone at the time. "We make more money in the other businesses. Why don't you get out of it?"

I truly felt that the business simply needed more time. We owned a lot of real estate in a variety of central and popular locations, which would only increase in value. We had to be patient. We had deeper pockets financially at this point and could afford to wait it out.

This was the same mindset we had needed to adopt when we got into self-storage in 2008. Matthew had found land in Dartmouth Crossing, a commercial real estate area in the Halifax municipal region. We built an $8 million facility with four hundred storage units. For the first few years, we lost money—at least $1 million within the first five. But we stuck it out. We knew we had to get to 70 percent occupancy of the storage lockers before we made a profit. Which we eventually did. About three years ago, we sold this storage facility to an American company for $13.5 million.

Any business can work if you have a decent concept and a good culture. Every company has its day if you run it correctly. With Moore Suites, we persevered through the rough years as well. Then, after the sale of Atlantic Signature Mortgage & Loan, I decided to step back from the business and put someone new in charge: Chris. He had made a great success of Atlantic Signature and was looking for what would be next. He wasn't keen on the suites business at this point, because we weren't making good money at it. "I'll try my best," he told me when he agreed to take the helm.

It was a very wise move on my part. I knew that he was more than capable. I had seen what he and Lizzie had done with Oceanstone. And Chris is very handy. He can fix anything, a perfect bonus when you're overseeing an accommodation business. His approach was successful. He cut costs (including reducing our inventory of suites from fifty-five to forty units), paid down our debt, and started turning profits.

We also faced the competition of Airbnb head-on. We could tell that the trend was not a flash in the pan. We had to learn how to live with it. One way was to insist on professionalism.

Many people complain about Airbnb rentals because clients often come in just to party and often have little respect for neighbours, not to mention the accommodations. In Waterfront Place, one of the buildings in Halifax where we had Moore Suites, we made sure someone from our company was on the residents' board so that we could be on call, ready to deal with any problems that came up with either our rental customers or with the building. There was reliability with Moore Suites. Customers knew what they were getting, which is not always the case with Airbnb. It can often be a huge disappointment that the accommodation doesn't look as nice as in the photographs online. We could eliminate the risk of customer disappointment. We chose great suites in good buildings—The Trillium, Salters Gate, Mary Queen of Scots Inn—often with a view of the water, in safe and pleasant neighbourhoods. And as always, we priced ourselves to be competitive.

In 2024, Chris and Lizzie bought my stake in the business to become full owners. Moore Suites now has forty units, generates $2 million in revenue, and is profitable. The company is also partnered in thirty long-term rental units with the Kanellakos family, well-known developers in Halifax.

Despite some rough years, we proved my hunch about the lucrative opportunity of the suites business. Hang on when your investment involves real estate. There are always solutions to a problem. In all, it was a satisfying conclusion to my adventure in the short-and-long-term accommodations business. With Moore Suites, I only ever wanted to create a small, sustainable, and profitable business, and that's precisely what Chris and Lizzie now have.

Chapter 11

Hard Lessons from Expensive Failures

Know your circle of competence, and stick within it. The size of that circle is not very important; knowing its boundaries, however, is vital.

WARREN BUFFETT

IT'S NOT ALL ROSES. I'VE DOCUMENTED A SERIES OF successes. But I'm the first to admit that I've had some doozy failures that cost me dearly. Entrepreneurs are dreamers and optimists. We're always on the lookout for opportunities. And we have big imaginations. A vision can unfold in a nanosecond. We pride ourselves on identifying an opportunity others might overlook.

But here's the truth. In entrepreneurship, there's no sure thing. It's a balance between weighing the risks and the potential benefits of an investment you're considering. On the one hand, you trust yourself. There will always be some people who are quick to highlight why some investment—or some vision—is not smart. They will call you a dreamer, suggesting you're not tethered to reality. They will repeat the adage: "If it sounds too good to be true, it probably is." So you learn to hear the naysayers but decide whether you want to pay attention to them. On the other hand, you have doubts. Of course you do. It's only natural. And I would argue that they're valuable. Give them space to expand. Examine the doubts. Do the homework. Research the sector you're interested in. Ask for advice. Pick an expert's brain.

But even then, when you have carefully considered the opportunity, there are still unknowns. And that's when you realize that you can't let hesitation and worry kill your tolerance of risk. Suspicion, cynicism, and fear keep many people from taking advantage of excellent opportunities. I have seen this phenomenon many times over.

Every investment opportunity comes to a hard point: decline or roll the dice.

Let me share a couple of cautionary tales.

In 2006, I first heard about Advance Commission, a payday loan provider for real estate agents, based in Kentville, Nova Scotia. Paul Burden, CA, who was the CEO, told me that Advance Commission was a prospering venture, with a growing roster of clients. Using its own capital and a line of credit, the company lent money to realtors when a real estate deal was executed. The loan would then be repaid with interest at the time of closing. Intriguing, don't you think? I saw this as a promising investment.

Paul was seeking new partners, because two of Advance Commission's original investors were exiting the company. I was interested. I shared the opportunity with Len McNeil, a retired chartered accountant with a master's degree in finance who had worked for Grant Thornton LLP, a leading Canadian accounting and advisory firm providing audit, tax, and advisory services to private and public organizations.

Len was on the hunt for investments. He had a financial interest in a trailer company in Truro, Nova Scotia, and in his retirement he was looking for more opportunities to boost his income.

It seemed like an obvious fit. Len's financial expertise gave me confidence in his ability to assess the opportunity.

"Make sure it's clean," I had said to Len before he went off to examine the opportunity. This was his living, so surely, he could spot any problems.

He came back after a week in Paul's office, where he had studied the company, looking at bank statements and financial overviews. "It's clean," he assured me.

I will never forget that moment. The rosy portrait of the company's prospects and financial position seemed correct. There was nothing to suggest that Paul was a shady character. In fact, he appeared to be a humble and kind family man. He and his wife weren't living an extravagant lifestyle.

In all, Len and I each put more than $1 million into Advance Commission to each secure a 20 percent stake in the company. Paul held the remaining 60 percent and ran the day-to-day operations.

For six years, right up until 2012, we were delighted with our investment. The company appeared to be profitable, expanding, and low risk. Money was rolling in. Len and I were both receiving quarterly interest payments equivalent to 12 percent of our investment—a great return—thus reducing the amount of our money tied up in the business.

But then, suddenly, the bubble burst. Len noticed a simple error on a financial statement sent by Paul, which had reportedly been audited by an accounting firm. The statement was improperly dated. Paul had put the wrong year on the statements when manipulating them. Len became immediately suspicious.

Quickly, the house of cards collapsed.

Paul soon admitted his fraud. For years he'd been heavily altering Advance Commission's financial statements, inflating revenue and earnings. In fact, it had been operating at a net loss since 2007. Every year, he brought in new investors, luring them in the same manner he had attracted us—with fraudulent financial statements. It was all a sham from the beginning. The funds we invested were merely used to buy out the original partners, making it a true Ponzi scheme.

In April 2015, Paul pled guilty to three counts of fraud and was sentenced to four years in jail. We were told that only a forensic accountant would have been able to detect the fraud at the outset. We were devastated. Shocked.

And I was heartbroken for Len when I learned that he and his wife, Anne, had put much of their net worth into the company. To come up with the $1 million initial investment, they had mortgaged their house and cottage and borrowed from RBC. Nearly all their personal assets were tied up as security on those loans.

As a Supreme Court of Nova Scotia judge later noted: "They were in very deep." I would never have taken the risk that Len did. And if I'd known that he was putting so much on the line, I would have tried to dissuade him.

The fraud was very costly to RBC, which had loaned Advance Commission millions of dollars. (That lending was separate from the RBC loans Len used to invest in the first place.) Overall, RBC lost about $9 million. I later learned that RBC's decision to loan the company money was partially influenced by its "comfort and knowledge of the three principals," including me. The bank saw my participation as a sign of safety. I lent Paul credibility.

Len and I, meanwhile, had both signed personal guarantees of $400,000, meaning we both owed that amount to RBC in addition to what we'd lost when the value of our shares evaporated. For me, the total loss was roughly $1.5 million.

In 2015, Len decided to sue RBC, alleging that the bank should have caught the fraud and shouldn't have continued to advance money to the company. He argued that RBC was negligent ("asleep at the switch") in its lending and should have had stricter controls to monitor Advance Commission's borrowing. He felt that RBC was responsible for his losses.

Len asked if I'd join his legal fight. It seemed possible that RBC might settle the suit out of court, which could reduce the amount each of us owed. Joining Len's lawsuit could potentially cut my losses by a couple of hundred thousand dollars. I sympathized with Len and understood that he wanted some retribution for the devastating loss he and his wife had suffered.

But there would be a cost, which I had to carefully consider if I were to join the lawsuit. First, lawsuits are hellish. Every effort should be made to avoid them. When you're entangled in a lawsuit, you think about it every day. You're losing money, energy, and time fighting a case you might not win. In the past fifty years, I have only been to court four times. Even during my time in the trucking business, where not a day passes without some sort of disagreement, I solved my problems without lawyers or the courts.

Second, if I joined Len's legal fight, I'd have to abandon my principles of fairness and responsibility. I'd signed the $400,000 personal guarantee. I took the risk. Put my name on the line. When you do that, you have to live with the consequences.

Third, if I sued the bank, my long-standing relationship with RBC would become strained, if not completely severed. That would include my rapport with Kim Mason, RBC's regional president in Atlantic Canada, whom I'd known for so long that I considered her a friend.

At the end of the day, I wasn't willing to make those sacrifices to save $200,000. I told Len that I wouldn't join him in his lawsuit. I felt badly for Len's losses. His financial situation was made much more precarious than mine by the loss. I had reserves of money. He did not. But I couldn't let that dissuade me from my decision. Every investor makes their own decisions.

As it turned out, the Supreme Court of Nova Scotia judge disagreed with Len's arguments and dismissed his claim. The judge noted that Len, despite his $1 million investment, never did the types of calculations or reviews that he argued RBC should have done. Simply put, Len sought to "impose a duty on RBC with respect to his investment that he himself was not willing to fulfill." Translation: RBC was not responsible for his losses.

My decision to make good on the $400,000 guarantee helped maintain—and perhaps even strengthen—my relationship with RBC. I don't know many people who will shed a tear for a Canadian bank, but I felt badly for RBC. I'd lent my name to Advance Commission, and we'd all been bitten by Paul's fraud. Running multiple businesses requires access to funding. It's critical to have a strong working relationship with your bank. By paying my debt, I preserved my bond with RBC and strengthened my reputation as someone who honours their commitments.

The judge in Len's lawsuit summed it up well when he wrote: "People are most likely to believe things that they most desperately want to be true. And everyone involved wanted Paul Burden's story to be true."

I think of myself as an excellent judge of character. And yet, I was taken in by Paul. He didn't seem like a Bernie Madoff character. His deception illustrates how difficult it is to truly know a person's inner thoughts and motivation. He later told me, when confronted, that he believed Advance Commissions would catch up and all the finances would eventually balance out. His Ponzi scheme was only a way to get more investors to jumpstart the company, he confessed to me. He desperately wanted to be a successful entrepreneur and clearly was willing to do anything to make success apparent. Talk about risks that entrepreneurs take. His were extreme and illegal.

Yup. It was one of those cases when if something sounds too good to be true, it probably is.

One of the obvious problems with Advance Commission was that neither Len nor I were involved with the day-to-day operations of the company. If you don't want to be closely connected to a business, stay out of it. Don't invest. I'm not saying that you have to be intimately involved in the day-to-day details of every business you invest in. But you should at least be regularly examining the financial statements and keeping in regular contact with upper management. It's an insight that many investors and entrepreneurs learn the hard way. Based on the size of the business, it's also critical to get professionally audited statements.

Worse—I've said I'm not perfect!—I had already learned this lesson in a previous failed investment in a nursing home business called Healthview.

That investment began with a pitch from David Riches, a chartered accountant with Grant Thorton who'd managed my finances for eight years. David was a friend. I trusted him deeply. He wanted me to join him as a partner in Healthview, a private nursing home business with eight nursing homes located in small Ontario towns with a total of about five hundred beds.

It seemed to be a solid proposal. Canada's aging population would boost demand. We'd have no difficulty securing clients. David had spent the previous six months researching the opportunity and the larger industry. He seemed to have a solid understanding of how to run the business. Plus, Peter McFadden, another skilled chartered account at David's firm, planned to leave his practice to run the business day-to-day. With David and Peter, I had little doubt that my investment was in safe, competent hands.

The offer was for me to join as a minority shareholder, owning between 5 and 10 percent of the shares. Even though David's pitch had appeal, I waffled when considering it. It was financially risky. We'd have $10 million in real estate liabilities and would have to sign personal guarantees for $2 million.

More significant was that the nursing home sector was well outside my field of expertise. I understand the service industry as well as anyone and, with small exceptions, I've stuck to that field. The service provided in each business may differ, but the underlying principles of the industry are the same; good service is good service, regardless of the business model. AMJ Campbell, Premiere Executive Suites, Moore Suites, Atlantic Signature Mortgage & Loan, and Oceanstone were very different businesses, but each one was a spoke within the larger wheel of the service industry. Plus, I knew those companies inside and out.

I'd never worked a single day or shift in a nursing home. And the fact is that a nursing home company is managed very differently than a moving company or a suites business. Nursing homes are administration-heavy, reliant on government funding, and overly bureaucratic. They are completely different than all my previous businesses and investments. It was a complex deal that I didn't fully understand.

I should have declined David's partnership offer. Instead, I suggested that I would likely invest and asked for an extra week to make a final decision. Bernardine and I were headed to Florida for vacation. I told David and Peter that I'd make a definitive call on the proposal by the time I returned.

Then, a terrible tragedy struck that swayed my thinking.

David died suddenly. He was in his fifties.

I was devastated over the loss. David was a wonderful guy and a dear friend. His accidental death should have immediately quashed the nursing home proposal. It had been David's idea and passion project from the beginning. Without his involvement, we should have shelved it.

Instead, that's when I made my crucial, ill-advised error. I let emotion govern my decision. Rather than viewing David's pitch rationally, with a clear-eyed business focus, I saw it as a way of honouring my friend. I could help bring his big idea to fruition. This may sound like an honourable intention, but it was a terrible reason to pursue the project.

I went ahead and paid $500,000 for a 25 percent stake in the business, an increase from my initial commitment of 5–10 percent. I also recruited my brothers Terry and Ted to join as fellow minority shareholders with about 20 percent, combined. Meanwhile, Peter McFadden, Healthview's CEO, held 45 percent.

Looking back on this investment, I see a few factors that doomed it. The management of any business is paramount to its success. In this case, Peter was a skilled chartered account, but he'd never run a business before. It's fair to say that he was shocked by the challenges of running a nursing home business at that time in Ontario. We faced labour and operational issues that are expected in any business, but our situation was complicated by the sector's bureaucracy.

The care our homes provided—which varied resident to resident—was covered by government. We'd made plans and projections based on the assumption that per-resident rates would increase—perhaps not by much, but at least by an amount tethered to inflation.

Instead, a newly elected NDP government (no friend of business, on a good day) froze rates, thus capping our revenue and rendering our projections useless. Government-run nursing homes already received about 30 percent more per resident than private homes like ours. The NDP government also added new regulations to the industry, including a boost to the amount of overhead each home had to spend per patient. They insisted on more hours from nursing staff per patient. We were forced to hire more people to fulfill these mandates.

Our unionized workforce compounded the problems. A 4–5 percent annual pay increase was expected despite our stagnant revenue from government. This represented yet another reason why I should never have invested in the business. As I've noted earlier in this book, I'm anti-union and much prefer to deal with employees on an individual basis, with the ability to reward hard work, not mere seniority.

As well, the value of our highly leveraged real estate dipped, forcing us to refinance our properties and add further personal guarantees. I had to guarantee an additional $300,000. I was now personally on the hook for $700,000 in guarantees.

I wanted out. My brothers wanted out. Peter was so shaken by the experience that he was despondent. I didn't have the time or the inclination to get involved in the management of the company. I would have had to circumvent the government regulations somehow. As the company sank, Peter was nearly bankrupted. He asked for an entire year off! I had to talk him off the figurative ledge. Again, this anecdote reveals the stress entrepreneurs face.

Within two or three years, we sold the business for a mere dollar, just to be rid of it. Unfortunately, selling the business did not allow us to escape the company's crippling liabilities (real estate liabilities and a line of credit) which totalled $3.5 million. The granular details of how I finally exited the business aren't important. Suffice it to say that it was an acrimonious process that involved lawyers, lawsuits, and threats of more lawsuits. The lowest point came when our bank gave us just twenty-four hours to repay our $1.8-million line of credit—an absurd and unprofessional demand! The upshot is that I eventually settled my share of the liabilities for about $750,000. With legal fees, I lost about $1 million on my nursing home adventure.

The experience taught me very important and very expensive lessons: don't invest in businesses you don't understand and don't have the time or willingness to learn more about. If you aren't willing to be hands-on (or at least close to a business), don't be surprised when you lose money.

Do I regret these decisions? Well, yes, of course. Who wants to lose significant money? But hindsight is 20/20, just like they say. At the time, I believed I was doing the right thing.

Still, I felt like an utter failure as the investment crumbled. I questioned my instincts. I wondered if success and wealth had gone to my head, causing me to make poor decisions. I even thought that God had sent this trouble my way to teach me a lesson.

Not long after the nursing home disaster, I attended a Catholic retreat with a group of men that was led by two priests. This is something I do on occasion as I have always maintained a spiritual practice. It would be surprising to a lot of people to see the pain many men carry in their inner lives. It was an eye-opener for me. Whether it was about finances, economic hardships, family troubles, health, or the relationship between fathers and sons, the anguish many men feel is real. Yet, mostly it's carried in silence. We just don't show it in regular life, largely because of societal expectations that men remain stoic and in control of their feelings. I wonder if many men divulge all their doubts and worries to their closest friends—or wives.

At this particular retreat, the ritual was that a "talking stick" was passed around, and each participant spoke about his innermost fears and feelings. It was like a group confession. Very cathartic, and very humbling.

When it was my turn, I spoke about my utter disappointment in myself—this supposedly successful entrepreneur whom many admired but who had just made a terrible business decision. I was wrangling with the banks at the time to bring the whole thing to an end. It was a very stressful time, and it felt good to air the problem in a group. The other men were sympathetic and supportive. I sat back, feeling better, and passed the stick to the next man. He had terminal cancer. With great courage, he talked about how he was managing the prognosis, his fears for his family, his imminent death, his faith in God.

I was deeply struck by his grace. I came home to Bernardine, who was the one to often bear the brunt of my disappointments. She had encouraged me to go to the retreat.

"I have no problems," I told her. "We're lucky. Problems are relative."

We hugged and talked through my experience at the retreat. Bernardine has always been a stalwart and patient partner with a vast amount of forbearance for my crazy energy.

I had grown up. I had made a mistake. I was lucky to have been in a position where the losses didn't decimate my net worth. I could afford to make mistakes. Which isn't true for others.

In a fifty-year business career, it's impossible to avoid failure completely. A quote from Tom Watson Sr., the chair and CEO of IBM, brilliantly summarizes my approach to investing since the nursing home debacle: "I'm no genius. I'm smart in spots—but I stay around those spots." Henry Ford was no stranger to failure. "Failure is simply the opportunity to begin again, this time more intelligently," he famously said.

Any seasoned entrepreneur can tell you at least one horror story about an investment they'd like to recoup.

The key is to not be discouraged. Pick yourself up. Brush yourself off. And carry on.

Chapter 12

Not Every Battle is Worth Fighting

He will win who knows when to fight and when not to fight.

SUN TZU

The Art of War

DISPUTES, DISSENSION, AND CONFLICT ARE UNAVOIDABLE in entrepreneurship. I've certainly had my share. The key is learning how to survive. That includes having thick skin and knowing how to negotiate. There are few people who will cause me to back down. I pride myself on my toughness that didn't come naturally but which I developed over fifty years of navigating various businesses, deals, investments—and difficult people! Inner toughness will help you manage trying situations without losing your cool or your sanity. I know how to win.

That doesn't mean you have to play dirty or be heartless to succeed in business, despite the stereotype of the cold CEO who makes decisions based only on the bottom line with no regard for other people, the planet, or basic decency. You do not have to be like Trump. It is possible to be a nice guy and finish first if you have your priorities clearly in mind.

Nonetheless, an important skill is also knowing when a battle is lost and not worth any more of your time, energy, or capital. You often have to pick which battles are worth fighting. That's not a sign of weakness. Rather it's a strength knowing what really matters to you. Let me tell you a story that illustrates one of the battles I happily lost.

The Crane Resort, built in 1887, is the oldest continuously operating hotel in the Caribbean and one of the most famous. Located on the rugged, rocky Atlantic side of Barbados, the Crane is in the town of St. Philip, about an hour's drive from the capital, Bridgetown. In its early days, the resort became a hideout for the world's elite. "Buffalo Bill" Cody famously paid for his room charges by leaving behind his gold chain and fob watch. Back then the Crane was an eighteen-room hotel. Under the ownership of Canadian Paul Doyle, who first visited in 1988, it has expanded to include suites and condos, with five swimming pools and four restaurants.

For years, two friends of mine, lawyer Peter Green and Larry Smith, lawyer and the former CFL commissioner, insisted that Bernardine and I visit Barbados and stay at the Crane. We turned them down multiple times, however, explaining that we weren't beach people. We were avid skiers.

In 2000, we finally relented and booked a stay at the Crane mainly because the resort had started selling time-share condos. I thought this could add nicely to our roster of properties at Premiere Executive Suites, which I was running at the time. Bernardine and I are seasoned travellers, and yet we were both stunned by what we found there: beautiful grounds, a charming plantation-style hotel with wooden floors and high ceilings, and rooms with wood-shuttered French windows that opened onto the turquoise sea, water pounding the rocks below.

At the end of our two-week stay, we paid US$54,000 for fractional ownership of a time-share condo, for personal and business use.

Two years later, on another visit, I noticed a neighbouring property—home of the modest Sunrise Beach Apartments—that looked ripe for redevelopment. We chatted with the owner, a lovely lady in her early eighties named Lurline, and I eventually asked if she was interested in selling. She explained that many people had approached her with similar queries, but she'd always turned them away because she didn't want to leave the property. I sensed that Lurline could be persuaded to sell with the right offer. If she sold to me, I told her, she could continue to live on the property for the rest of her life—rent free. My offer piqued her interest, and she said she'd give it serious thought. Good to her word, she did, although it took a few months for her to finally agree to a sale. I agreed to pay US$800,000 for the Sunrise Beach property, lined up investors, and began drafting plans for our redevelopment of the property.

I believed there was an opportunity for a new competitor to enter the market. I envisioned a landmark property where I could leverage my extensive knowledge of the service industry: an extended-stay hotel of perhaps forty suites, with a restaurant, bar, and pool.

Shortly before our deal with Lurline closed, she told me that another neighbour, John Lashley, might also be interested in selling his property, which was about half the size of hers and had a dilapidated house on it. His asking price was US$500,000, but he agreed to my offer of US$450,000. Although I didn't need the second property to fulfill my development vision, I decided to personally buy it. With deals on two properties about to close, I felt comfortable with respect to the investment.

But that's as far as my plans would go. I was about to encounter the opposite of renowned Barbadian hospitality.

A month after accepting my offer (and my US$7,500 deposit), John Lashley suddenly claimed that he didn't want to sell after all. One of his neighbours was unhappy with my purchase of two properties. The neighbour was another Canadian: Eugene Melnyk, the pharmaceutical billionaire and owner of the Ottawa Senators. He held extensive property on the island, including a $25 million estate adjacent to the two properties I was eyeing for redevelopment.

Turns out that Eugene had been buying much of the land around his estate in an effort to insulate his property (and his neighbours) from development. My recent deals conflicted with that plan. You might assume that the involvement of another Canadian would have helped smooth the situation and lead to a Canuck compromise. Hardly. I consider myself a savvy businessman and a skilled negotiator, but even I wasn't prepared for my dealings with Eugene.

Eugene, who died in 2022 at age sixty-two, was a rich bully who plowed through people to get what he wanted. In this case, he wanted my properties, and he was going to get them. Period. When he heard about my plan to buy the two properties, he quickly applied pressure, hoping to scuttle the sales. Lurline told me that Eugene offered her and John Lashley each an extra US$50,000 if they quashed their deals with me and sold to him instead. To her immense credit, Lurline turned him down. John, meanwhile, tried to get out of our deal.

I refused to budge. We had an agreement, and I believed he should honour it. (If the situation had been reversed, I certainly would have.) Eventually, I decided that I didn't need John's property to achieve my development goals. I met with Eugene, and after some unpleasant negotiation I agreed to back out of that deal in exchange for US$100,000. It was the fastest hundred grand I ever made.

That settled one battle. But another one loomed. Unfortunately, my purchase of Lurline's property had angered Eugene *and* Paul Doyle, the owner of the Crane. Now there were three Canadians fighting over a low-rise motel property thousands of kilometres from Canada. Neither guy wanted me to redevelop the property. So they employed various tactics to scare me off. At the same time, they were suing each other over separate, minor disagreements, catching me in a pissing match between two rich Canadians over a modest Caribbean property.

The land I bought from Lurline overlooked the famous Crane beach on the same cliff above the rocky southeast coast. At one point, Eugene called me from his private plane (clearly trying to impress me) and told me that a geological fracture ran under my property and the Crane, and that the Crane restaurant would crumble into the ocean within two years. I asked to see the geological study but, of course, he never produced it. (Twenty years later, I'm still waiting for Eugene's prediction to come true.)

Paul Doyle used a different, more aggressive intimidation tactic. A dead-end road ran across my property and ended at a rock wall on the border of the Crane Resort. The road hadn't been used in a decade so I'd torn part of it up to begin landscaping work. Paul, of course, knew this and suddenly tore down the rock wall separating our properties so that traffic could again flow along the road—and over my new landscaping work.

I was back in Chester when John Scherer, one of my partners, called me in a panic. Doyle had sent thirty-five construction workers onto my property to tear up my landscaping and repave the road—even though it hadn't been used in more than a decade! I told John to put our Land Rover in front of the rock wall to block our land off from Doyle's. Half an hour later, John called me again, even more agitated than before. The workers were paving around the Land Rover!

I knew then that this was a losing battle. Paul and Eugene were playing puerile, dirty tricks and clearly would use whatever threats or tactics necessary to get what they wanted. Normal business practices and ethics were irrelevant in this standoff.

I'm not a quitter, but there comes a time in every conflict where you must weigh your goals against the cost of winning. In this case, the cost of winning was very high—financially and mentally. I decided that my redevelopment plans weren't worth the money or mental anguish.

In October 2004, I talked to Eugene and agreed to sell. He directed me to his head lawyer and arranged a meeting at the Mississauga head office of his pharmaceutical company, Biovail. The lawyer was professional and courteous, yet he made it plain that I shouldn't fight Eugene.

Picking up his pen, the lawyer drew a circle on a piece of paper, with a dot in the middle.

"Do you know what this is?" he asked me.

"No."

"This is Eugene's sandbox. And Tim, you're in his sandbox." He arched an eyebrow at me. "You don't want to be in there."

It was an explanation fit for a preschooler. And very effective. I was furious, but by meeting's end we'd negotiated a deal. Eugene got Lurline's former property in exchange for what I'd paid for it, plus $250,000 to cover renovations I'd already made. (Lurline stayed, but passed away about a year later.) The agreement meant that I was able to extricate myself without taking a financial hit. Still, it was a deflating loss. It seemed like my vision of a Barbadian tourism property was dead.

But another twist in the tale lay ahead, proving the adage that when one door closes, another one opens. Or to put it another way: some battles that you lose lead to opportunities you wouldn't otherwise have seen.

John Scherer had identified an old house on a plot of land on the other side of the Crane. The land was right on the cliff's edge. The grass was wild and overgrown. The house was not inviting. But we saw potential.

"We can make this look wonderful," Bernardine said, looking around. She has a great eye for design and had helped decorate the units for Premiere Executive Suites.

We paid US$550,000 for the property and an old house and set out to realize our vision—free of conflict with our rich neighbours. The results have exceeded our expectations. We executed a major renovation on the existing house, which took one and a half years. That's Cragmere, a five-bedroom villa. On a vacant lot across the street, we built a 4,300 square-foot four-bedroom villa named Windermere. They are both run as separate rental businesses. The Cragmere rents through Moore Suites. Windermere was sold to Jason Hughes in London, England. He owned and rented it out for about four years. When he decided to sell three years ago, I contacted Leo Thibodeau, a friend of mine and former employee who loves Barbados. I have known him since he started working at AMJ Campbell as a teenager in the late 1980s. He now owns and rents out the property.

Each villa boasts ocean views from nearly every room, an infinity pool, plunge pool, expansive kitchen with granite countertops, coral accents everywhere, full concierge service, the option of a personal chef for all dinners, and an ensuite bathroom in every bedroom. (Chris proposed to Lizzie on the point jutting out from the Cragmere.)

It's no surprise that our profile on Tripadvisor is flooded with five-star reviews and, similar to Oceanstone, our Barbados properties have won many tourism awards.

Now, hold on, because the story gets better.

In the early 2010s, I was on the phone with Jason Buchanan, one of my closest business partners in Premiere Van Lines. He was busy pushing a dolly at the hospital in Kentville, Nova Scotia, where he was overseeing a big moving job.

Realizing that I was calling from the paradise of Barbados, Jason cut me off and jokingly asked, "How did this happen? We're partners but I do all the work, and you have all the fun."

I laughed. "You have to pay your dues," I assured him. He was a young guy.

In 2005, I'd recruited Jason away from his manager's position at RBC, convincing him to buy 46 percent of the struggling Halifax franchise of Premiere Van Lines, for a couple hundred thousand dollars. After the deal closed, Jason—who had no experience in the moving industry—asked me, "Tim, why me?"

"I just feel this energy," I replied. My gut told him that he's a natural for the job. His father had been an entrepreneur, and he always felt that he should be one, too. "I know you're going to work hard. I know that this partnership is going to be really successful."

And it was, although initially Jason was, in his words, "shitting bricks," unsure if he'd made the right decision. He struggled to make payroll, but he is a quick thinker and a hard worker, with a strong background in finance. He expanded into office moving and proved himself a local leader in that field by moving an entire 350-employee law firm between offices in a single weekend. He eventually pushed annual revenue from $2.5 million to $12 million, making it the largest moving company east of Montréal, with commercial transport clients such as Costco, Wayfarer, and Best Buy. I installed Jason as president of Premiere Van Lines in 2006 and later formed a partnership with him at Premiere Self Storage.

Over the years, I hounded Jason about visiting Barbados—much as my two lawyer friends had done with me before my first trip to the Crane Resort.

I told him multiple times: "You have to get down here. It's the most beautiful part of the world. This would be a perfect property for you to buy into."

At that point, Jason didn't have the funds necessary to invest in a property he'd only use for a few weeks of the year. By 2021, however, that had changed—we'd sold our stakes in both Premiere Van Lines (resulting in a twenty times return on Jason's initial investment) and our self-storage business. The result: Jason was a multi-millionaire.

Coincidently, John, my long-time partner in Barbados, was spending less time on the island and wanted to exit the business. It was excellent timing for Jason and me to buy all of John's stake in the business.

I offered Jason a third of the Barbados property for US$600,000, and he agreed despite having never seen or stayed at the Cragmere. There was enormous trust between us. It was a lovely way for a valuable partner to have realized the benefits of hard work.

In my encounters with Eugene Melnyk and Paul Doyle, I knew that battle was lost. But my experience in Barbados has been better than if I had won that war. Our subsequent Barbados investment has been a true highlight of my career and in our enjoyment as a family. I couldn't have imagined it in the middle of the fight with Eugene and Paul, but as it turned out, I was glad I backed out. Glad that I lost. Because in the end, I won something bigger.

Chapter 13

Feeding and Taming the Media Beast

Public relations is a mix of journalism, psychology, and lawyering—it's an ever-changing and always interesting landscape.

RONN TOROSSIAN

Founder of New York-based 5W Public Relations

IN THE 1980S, DURING THE DECADE OF AMJ CAMPBELL'S WILD expansion across the country, I was interviewed live on *Venture*, the CBC Television award-winning business program with an audience of 2 million. It was a show with similar clout as CBS's *60 Minutes*.

How did this come about? I approached *Venture* because I was unhappy that AMJ Campbell wasn't allowed to go to tender for moving contracts from Imperial Oil. The energy company did five hundred moves a year. Big business. I had asked for an opportunity to bid, but I was denied. They only went to tender with the big van lines, and AMJ Campbell was considered an agent within a van line, Atlas, so we weren't on the list.

This didn't sit well with me. Imperial Oil prided itself on fostering opportunity and entrepreneurialism. AMJ was unique. And we were just like a major van line. We had operations coast to coast. And we had greater flexibility in price. I knew this could be a great business story. And I bet that the media would be game to report on it.

Which they did.

The CBC recorded me on a phone call in my office with Imperial Oil as I made my pitch, asking for an opportunity at a moving contract and explaining the benefits of working with AMJ Campbell. When I was interviewed by Robert Scully, the show host, I was sincere and professional about the issue. AMJ was a burgeoning and exciting business, a true Canadian success story. Why were we being denied the chance to bid? I was simply laying out my grievance.

Later, after the segment aired, I heard that there had been internal discussions at Imperial Oil about suing my company for reputational damage. But that didn't bother me in the least. I was just asking for an opportunity. *Okay, sue me*, I thought. Big Imperial Oil suing a company like ours? It would have been stupid for them to do that. I had been keen to make a point. And I certainly wasn't timid.

Imperial Oil never sued us. As a result of that CBC interview, AMJ Campbell imprinted its name on the national business consciousness. It was a form of very effective branding. Free advertising! I was underscoring the ambition and professionalism of AMJ Campbell, a homegrown moving company that deserved a chance. People listened. We were the feisty underdog.

For a year, we got none of Imperial Oil's business. But after that year, AMJ bid on their commercial contract. And we landed it. That was a start. Years later, we also got most of their residential moving jobs.

You have to fight when you have to fight. Put yourself out there. And you need a good handle on how to feed—and sometimes tame—the media beast.

I lived and breathed all my companies. And with AMJ Campbell, in particular, I was relentless about media attention to increase our visibility and name recognition. I wanted seven out of ten people in a county to know our national company. That may seem ambitious, but I actively went after any attention, all attention. In Toronto, I bought a thirty-six-foot yacht and flew a huge AMJ flag on it to have a presence, cruising up and down the city's busy waterfront boardwalk.

In 1986, after being profiled in Allan Gould's book *The New Entrepreneurs: 80 Canadian Success Stories*, I kept in touch with him. He was writing for business magazines, and I'd pitch stories to him, which he often covered. Then, in 2003, *Profit* magazine called me to do a story about Premiere Executive Suites. Luckily, they commissioned Allan to write the story. He had identified me in the early days as an up-and-coming entrepreneur, so he was naturally interested in my evolution as I moved on to new things such as Premiere Executive Suites. In the *Profit* magazine article, titled "Mr. Nice Guy," I described how I was drawing on my success with AMJ to parlay the same approach into a new venture.

Reporters in mainstream, legacy media have to be objective, of course, and they're also super competitive. They benefit from close relationships with business leaders and their "sources." It's in their interest to develop close, trusted relationships with us. They will meet for drinks, for lunch, but not in a way that compromises their integrity. They want to talk. That's how they get stories no other outlet has. It's where they hear gossip that may lead to their next big scoop.

It's smart to pursue media relationships. But recognize that they take time to develop into trusted ones. Reporters can be tricky. They're sniffing you out, and you're assessing them. But be aware: It would be a mistake to think that you can pull the wool over a reporter's eyes. They're never really going to be a great friend, not while they're writing for media outlets. And if they say they want an off-the-record discussion, only participate once you're sure you can trust them—and they have no recording device on!

I have always been my own public relations person. I never hired a firm to handle media. I knew my business. I was proud of everything we achieved. I didn't have anything to hide. And because I like people, I made a point of finding a connection with reporters and developing my network.

I also believed that there were interesting aspects to business growth and entrepreneurship that others would find useful as well as cautionary. That's the former teacher in me, I guess. I wrote two books prior to this one. I have given lots of speeches, often describing the funny anecdotes of my business life. I have thick files of media stories in my office. Hundreds of them. And I framed some of the articles to put on my office walls.

Of course, my tenure during the crazy growth years of my businesses and new ventures came before the advent of social and digital media, which dominates marketing and public image these days. But what social media does now—give readers an inside behind-the-scenes look at the personality responsible for the brand—I was doing in traditional media at the time. Bernardine didn't always like the publicity I encouraged, especially about features on our house. She likes her privacy. But she went along with it, out of support for adding to our corporate profile.

People care about a business venture, but it's the people who make it interesting. Isn't that why people fixate on Gwyneth Paltrow regarding her brand, Goop? Or Jeff Bezos of Amazon? Or Steve Jobs of Apple? Not that I was ever in their celebrity stratosphere, but I was the personality of the AMJ brand, of Premiere Executive Suites, of Atlantic Signature, of Oceanstone, of Moore Suites. I was the go-to media contact. I was proud of my visibility, and I pursued it. I stuck out in the way I did business, in the way I dressed, and in the honesty I employed when dealing with reporters. I was there to tell it like it is.

I would be the first one to call up a reporter to describe a challenge such as the time when I felt a little overwhelmed with the accommodation business at Premiere Executive Suites. I wasn't about to sugarcoat the challenges of a novice running what felt like a hotel. Reporters and social media followers want to hear what *doesn't* go well as much as about what does go according to plan. It's important to understand your audience and to provide content that's authentic and gritty.

Many business leaders worry about projecting perfection. And the truth is, many successful entrepreneurs are held up as iconic. Often, as a result, they want their brand to appear effortlessly wonderful and popular. I've heard people warn that a business owner should never admit when things are slow or not going well. "Project success!" they often advise; suggest that everything is great, even when it's not. And while I agree that you have to remain positive and have a solution to a problem, I also think that it's smart to acknowledge the difficulties at times. We all know running a business and developing it into a success is not a cakewalk.

Lately, perhaps because of the cultural acknowledgement of mental health issues and the need to openly address them, several digital entrepreneurs have discussed their struggles. Toby Thomas, CEO of EnSite Solutions, describes the entrepreneur's mental outlook with a great analogy of a man riding a lion. "People look at him and think, 'This guy's really got it together. He's brave!' And the man riding the lion is thinking, 'How the hell did I get on a lion, and how do I keep from getting eaten?'" So perfect! So true!

This openness about mental health is driven by the younger generation, and I applaud it. I read a statistic recently that 7.5 out of 10 venture-backed tech start-ups fail, according to Shikhar Ghosh, a Harvard Business School professor. And the majority fall short of their projections. Two out of 10 businesses fail in the first year of operations, says the Bureau of Labour. Only 1 percent of start-ups become so-called unicorn firms like Uber, Airbnb, Slack, Stripe, and Docker, according to CB Insights.

My faith has helped me in my struggles. We all need to seek help when we're disappointed in ourselves or meet with embarrassing failures. I have also found that treating yourself is important, whether that be travel or buying something you want. In 1995, I bought my first Rolls-Royce to reward myself for all the hard, back-breaking work in the early days—and that was a financial stretch then. But it helped keep me going.

As entrepreneurs, we are walking and talking human-interest stories. People are interested in business founders who take risks, make tough decisions, and sometimes have poor judgment. They want to follow them. Triumph over adversity is far more interesting than the story of someone who pretends that they swanned into success without hitting any potholes. Change is what business is about. Doing something new for the marketplace. Realizing where you've made mistakes. Backtracking on decisions, if necessary. Acknowledging your weaknesses. Admitting failure. Coming up with a fresh idea. Figuring out how to pivot when needed. Confessing to regrets for not having followed through on some opportunity you gave up on.

Entrepreneurship is a fluid, dynamic endeavour; a dramatic story of human emotions—ambition, hope, regret, satisfaction, pride. Be that story. Expose and embrace your humanity.

One of the best examples I can offer is how I dealt with *Frank* magazine. The satirical magazine is widely read even though many people profess not to, as though juicy gossip is beneath them. The writers and editors at *Frank* are out to prick the balloons of political and corporate egos. They often want to embarrass their subjects.

Over the years, they have taken plenty of shots at my business peers, but they never set their sights on me. I have been mentioned over two dozen times in their pages. Sure, my house was listed a few times in their compilations of Chester's biggest homes (they once called ours the "most prestigious house in Chester"), but *Frank* never criticized or lampooned me for my behaviour in business or in my personal life. I draw great pride from that.

Why did *Frank* seem to give me a pass? I believe there are a few reasons. I've always run clean, professional operations. My businesses never produced scandals and blunders that make for great tabloid fodder. I treat people well, and deal with problems head-on and without delay, not allowing small issues to transform into public spectacles. And if a reporter called me, I usually offered to meet them for coffee or lunch. I would ignore the advice of others who told me not to engage, especially with *Frank* magazine.

"I love to put a face to a name," I'd say to the reporter.

So, what's the best strategy? Disarm reporters. They're accustomed to having people ignore their calls. Meet them. Sit down with them. Be natural. Have a sense of humour. Talk to them. Remember, if they want to do a story about you, and you refuse to co-operate, they'll find a way by going around you. They will talk to anonymous sources, enemies, and allies. It is best to have your side explained. Have your say. Set the record straight if you want. But never forget: reporters have the last word because they're the ones writing the story. Don't think you can completely control the outcome. Thicken your skin.

One last note. If there's a major controversy that you're involved in, which you'd rather see disappear, I have another great piece of media advice. It's very simple. Don't feed the beast. The story will fade. Some new shiny story will attract their attention tomorrow or the next day or next week. Remain in dignified silence.

Chapter 14

Money Matters

Financial peace isn't the acquisition of stuff. It's learning to live on less than you make, so you can give money back and have money to invest. You can't win until you do this.

DAVE RAMSEY

The Total Money Makeover

I WANT TO TALK ABOUT MONEY. FEW PEOPLE LIKE DISCUSSING it, perhaps because it makes them uncomfortable or insecure. But let's be honest. Money is loaded with meaning. Some people might consider a discussion about money to be déclassé. Were you brought up to believe that it wasn't polite to talk about money?

In some ways, one could argue that money is the last taboo. It used to be that sex was taboo, never to be discussed. But look at our culture now: Explicit sex images are everywhere. Articles and books discuss sexual behaviours like they're table manners with specific instructions.

Money should be demystified. It can affect your life and well-being. I have had to learn to manage it and understand it. The underlying messages of money are important to recognize. Some use it as a substitute for love and attention. It is a way to show praise by offering it for a job well done and to mete out punishment by withholding it. Money confers status and power. Unfortunately, it is often how people measure others. Some people hate it. Some people love it and always want more of it.

Money is an energetic current that runs through everyone's life, no matter how you feel about it. So, in my view, it's important to take stock of your relationship with it. Do you hoard it? Do you overspend it? You do fear it? Do you avoid it? Are you comfortable asking for a raise at work? I think there's big business in being a money shrink because we all have an individual attitude about it based on our psychological makeup, our background—and our gender. Women, in particular, can find money discussions difficult. Suze Orman, a podcaster, pundit, and bestselling author of financial books, has unravelled the complexities of women and money issues. When you understand your particular dynamic about money matters, you can make the most of what it makes possible—for yourself and others.

Like any person, and as a good businessman, I don't like to spend money unnecessarily. I don't care how rich you are, if a charge seems unfair, you shouldn't pay it. Having said that, I am not the type of person who scrutinizes every single bill to discern the value. I don't refuse to pay restaurant bills if the meal is poor, for example. If I didn't like the service or the food, I simply won't go again. A simple solution.

With other bills, just because you have the money to pay an exorbitant amount doesn't mean you should feel obliged to pay it if it's unfair. Many people think that when someone is wealthy, they don't worry or pay attention to their money. I would say the exact opposite is true. Take, for instance, Ken Thomson. One of the richest men in Canada, he was well known in Toronto's Rosedale circles for buying day-old bread at Summerhill Market. It's just as good as fresh bread—and cheaper! Why not?

I am comfortable questioning a bill if I have a problem with it. I ask the person who issued it to explain the costs. Some people might think that it would be embarrassing to complain about a bill. Will they think you're broke? Scrooge-like? No. They'll think you pay attention to costs. They'll appreciate that you understand value. You have to find your own sense of whether it's appropriate or not to complain.

Bernardine remains very frugal as a matter of habit. She's not keen on buying expensive clothes and jewellery. If she sees something on the curb that someone has thrown out, she will get out of the car and have a look. And she'll take it if she likes it and finds it useful.

As a regular buyer and seller of real estate properties, I often come up against interest penalties that are routinely assessed when one discharges a mortgage early.

One such incident in the 1990s arose when a penalty from the Royal Bank was $6,000. Wendy Langlois was my bank manager at the time, who later came to work for me at AMJ Campbell. I told Wendy flat out: "I don't want to pay that." I had given them a lot of business over the years, and felt I could be straightforward.

There was a beat of silence on the other end of the phone. "I'm really sorry," she replied eventually, clearly somewhat taken aback. "I can do a lot of things around here. But this is definitely not one of them." I could tell that she was not expecting this from me. And I must admit, I'm a little harder on banks than most people. My relationship with Wendy had always been friendly and productive. She reiterated that there was nothing she could do. Bank policy, she said.

I would not accept her refusal to amend this charge. I asked her politely to consult the head office.

Perhaps she was insulted that I wanted to go over her head to her superiors. I don't know. I simply stated my objection and wanted it addressed. Bank policy is neither a good answer nor good for customer relations.

She conceded.

A few days later, Wendy called me back. "You owe me big time!" she laughed. "The penalty has been waived." She was surprised by her own bank's decision. And maybe she learned something important about flexibility and the opportunity to placate and accommodate good customers. Many banks nowadays are not so flexible with their willingness to circumvent rules. But you should never forget that you are their valued customer, and they should listen to you if you're unhappy with something.

Banking people are business people. Just like lawyers. They can be intimidating. But they understand the importance of maintaining a happy relationship. They're in the service business, after all.

The complexity of our management of money also involves some interesting paradoxes. In my case, for example, I love making money, as I have said. I enjoy helping other people become wealthy. I will spend money lavishly on things Bernardine and I want, and on what my businesses need. I will take calculated risks with it on investments. I won't pay unwarranted bills, and I always ask for quotes.

And I really love giving money away. I have always felt compelled to give back, to give money for worthwhile causes. Philanthropy is a key business strategy. It builds a sense of community and shows an appreciation for the power of money that you have been blessed to accumulate and which you can now use to help others. Your brand value augments. You gain recognition. Philanthropy is a form of marketing, reinforcing a corporate culture that is inclusive, compassionate, and engaged. But more important, it brings profound meaning to work. I would even say it gives spiritual meaning to your professional life.

Every single business I've had in Canada has had a philanthropic policy. The focus has varied company to company, but there was always a clear understanding that we all must do our part and contribute to society. My AMJ Campbell moving company gave millions of dollars to different charities. The tradition is carried on today now giving approximately a million annually, according to Pierre Frappier, the new owner. After my mother died of cancer, and others that many of us knew also struggled or died from the disease, my companies had a strong calling to contribute to research and help in whatever ways we could. AMJ was privileged to become involved in the life of a specific cancer patient, Jean Ann Lewis, a young woman diagnosed with breast cancer that had spread to her liver. Despite a negative prognosis, she became a great inspiration at AMJ Campbell. Together with Bob Deluce of Deluce Investments (and Porter Airlines) and Doug McCutcheon of Rosedale Livery, we raised over $40,000 in a six-week period to send Jean to special therapy in the United States. The treatments helped stabilize the cancer. It was perhaps the most moving moment in the history of our company when she came to our office to thank our employees for "giving" her life. We were moved to tears.

Years later, at AMJ Campbell, when one of our highly respected franchisees and partners, Barb Lippai, died of cancer, we set up a national Barb Lippai Community Service Award to honour our most charitable office across Canada every year. Unfortunately, when I left AMJ Campbell, I learned that the award had been renamed in honour of Bruce Bowser. Understandably, that just underscored my great displeasure with him as my successor.

We sponsored sports teams and Olympians, and in Calgary my brother Terry helped up to twenty-five charities each year, including the annual Huron Carole, a nationally touring musical production that partners with Food Banks Canada and raises donations for local food banks. When severe flooding hit Manitoba, we provided trucks to ship clothes, food, and furniture required by flood victims. Across my companies, there are too many causes to name that we helped.

Philanthropy motivates your employees. People crave meaning; many studies show that philanthropic endeavours engage employees in a sense of social purpose. In particular, many in the younger generation are deeply committed to social justice and community. A philanthropic policy in your company can often be the reason people want to join, and stay with, your organization. I don't believe that anyone in business can succeed without giving back.

For Bernardine and me, altruism has been embedded in our DNA from the beginning. That's true for many in Canada. In 2023, Canadian tax filers reported a total of $12.8 billion in charitable donations, a significant increase of $1.4 billion compared to 2022. This increase was driven by a rise in the number of donors, particularly among those with incomes of $60,000 and over, according to Statistics Canada. And in the same year, 73 percent of Canadians engaged in formal and informal volunteering.

Personally, Bernardine and I have donated millions. And we have helped raise millions for worthy causes. Over the years, we have hosted thousands of guests to help raise money for organizations such as the Alzheimer Society, the Chester Playhouse, and the Stephen Lewis Foundation. One year we raised $107,000 in a single day for Stephen's foundation, with the funds supporting grassroots organizations in Africa that were fighting the spread of HIV/AIDS. Others include mental health groups, Saint Mary's University (where I was a board member for many years), King's-Edgehill private school (where I served on the board of governors), Canadian Museum of Immigration at Pier 21, and mental health charities including the Mental Health Foundation of Nova Scotia. We have donated stays in our Barbados villa in silent auctions for various charities for over twenty years, raising over $300,000 in the process.

In 2002, I was deeply honoured to receive the Queen's Golden and Platinum Jubilee Medals in recognition of my philanthropic work and "outstanding and exemplary contributions" to Canada. I feel this award is less about myself and more a tribute to all the good and kind employees that have worked for my companies.

Abraham Lincoln is famously attributed with the line, "When I do good, I feel good, when I do bad, I feel bad, and that's my religion." Don't we all wish in this fraught political moment that all American presidents subscribed to such a stance? To be sure, not everyone is governed by a sense of wanting to do what is right or good. But there's something heartening in the knowledge that for most people the act of giving to others, of helping others, is rewarded and encouraged by also making us feel good about ourselves. Thankfully, it is part of what defines us as a species. It makes us human.

Chapter 15

Find Your Sanctuary

Be true to yourself, help others, make each day your masterpiece, make friendship a fine art, drink deeply from good books...build a shelter against a rainy day, give thanks for your blessings and pray for guidance every day.

JOHN WOODEN
Basketball coach

I HAVE A FAVOURITE PASSAGE THAT I WANT TO SHARE because it helps explain an attitude about life that I have learned to adopt. It's taken from a poem titled "The Station" in *A Penny's Worth of Minced Ham: Another Look at the Great Depression* by Robert J. Hastings.

> *Tucked away in our subconscious minds is an idyllic vision in which we see ourselves on a long journey that spans an entire continent. We're traveling by train and, from the windows, we drink in the passing scenes of cars on nearby highways, of children waving at crossings, of cattle grazing in distant pastures, of smoke pouring from power plants, of row upon row upon row of cotton and corn and wheat, of flatlands and valleys, of city skylines and village halls.*

But uppermost in our conscious minds is our final destination—for at a certain hour and on a given day, our train will finally pull into the station with bells ringing, flags waving, and bands playing. And once that day comes, so many wonderful dreams will come true. So restlessly, we pace the aisles and count the miles, peering ahead, waiting, waiting, waiting for the station.

"Yes, when we reach the station, that will be it!" we promise ourselves. "When we're eighteen...win that promotion...put the last kid through college...buy that 450SL Mercedes-Benz...put the last kid through college...have a nest egg for retirement!"

From that day on, we will live happily ever after.

Sooner or later, however, we must realize there is no station in this life, no one earthly place to arrive at once and for all. The journey is the joy. The station is an illusion—it constantly outdistances us....

"Relish the moment" is a good motto, especially when coupled with Psalm 118:24, "This is the day which the Lord hath made; we will rejoice and be glad in it." It isn't the burdens of today that drive men mad, but regrets over yesterday and fear of tomorrow.

So stop pacing the aisles and counting the miles. Instead, swim more rivers, climb more mountains, kiss more babies, count more stars. Laugh more and cry less. Go barefoot oftener. Eat more ice cream. Ride more merry-go-rounds. Watch more sunsets. Life must be lived as we go along.

[Reprinted with the permission of Southern Illinois University Press.]

Long ago, I realized that my restlessness would never completely abate. Even when I met goals that I set and had great financial success, I still took on projects, new investments, and businesses. There never seemed to be a finish line. There was always more that I wanted to do. That is my nature. But along the way, I realized that Bernardine and I needed a sanctuary, a place that would be our still point, where we could find some calm and reset ourselves when needed.

I know many entrepreneurs who find a special place for this purpose. A cabin in the woods might be their bolthole, away from the cut and thrust of the business world. Or perhaps that sanctuary can be found in a cockpit at thirty thousand feet, flying a plane. Richard Branson and Jeff Bezos both focus on space exploration—with Virgin Galactic and Blue Origin, respectively—to get away from it all, in their cases, quite literally leaving the frustration of Earthly life far below.

Many entrepreneurs find a daily routine that helps them focus—or conversely, helps them zone out and recharge. Tony Robbins, inspirational speaker and bestselling author, starts each day with a cold plunge in fifty-six-degree water. Others meditate. I work out. My physical fitness, throughout my life, has been part of my discipline. I can ruminate about business problems while I exercise. I can also escape them when on the treadmill and lifting weights.

But more than anything else, what I needed in my life as an entrepreneur is a place like our home in Chester, Nova Scotia.

In the late 1980s, Bernardine and I, along with Chris and Matthew, were living in Toronto, a short commute from the AMJ Campbell head office in Mississauga. Those final years in Toronto had been both stressful and poignant. I was working like a madman, travelling all over the country. Meanwhile, my mother was dying of lung cancer. She rarely had to stay in hospital because Bernardine nursed, supported, and inspired her for two years in our home. We created a bedroom for her on the lower level of our house, which allowed easy accessibility. When my mother was in the latter stages of her illness, Bernardine would occasionally light a cigarette and hold it to my mother's mouth, providing her a small pleasure in her last days. My mother was always a serious smoker, so this act of compassion was one of her last enjoyments in life. I will always treasure Bernardine for the thoughtfulness and care she showed.

When my mother died, I wanted to rethink my life. This happens when a parent dies, I believe. A generation passes, and you're next, so of course, you examine your own mortality. My father died about ten years later. Thankfully, I had had the chance to reconcile with him after our strained relationship during my early years. He was extremely proud of me and my accomplishments, and we were able—finally—to have heartfelt conversations. I am very grateful for that, although I still feel that I fell short of what I could have done for him. I feel that I should have spent more time with him. But I was so busy with business and my own family. I think many people feel this way after they lose their parents. Time together is invaluable.

For years, Bernardine had been trying to convince me to move to the Maritimes. At this juncture, she could sense that I was craving change. I remember her telling me, "Tim, if you want water, I'll show you where there's lots of water! Try Nova Scotia." We also shared a desire to raise our boys in a small town, where they could safely walk and ride their bikes anywhere. Though Chester seemed to make sense, and I was losing my feeling of connection to Toronto, I was still hesitant. I told Bernardine I'd try it, but made her promise that we could move back to Ontario if I didn't like it. She agreed.

We had first visited Chester, which is located about sixty kilometres south of Halifax, during our honeymoon in 1977. We loved it. The seaside village, which has been called the "Riviera of the Maritimes," has a special, unspoiled charm that has wooed many people throughout history. Loyalists came north after the American Revolution to settle there. Later, in the mid-1900s, many Americans from New England, New York, and the surrounding areas, came to Chester for the summer. Some have called it "the poor man's Hamptons" because the real estate was less expensive than in similar communities on the Eastern Seaboard. Most notably, the Pew family of Pennsylvania, who made their fortune in the oil industry, spent the summers in Chester and became well known for their generosity to locals by donating a large tract of land on the sea to be converted into a golf course that everyone could afford to join. Wealthy visitors from all over the world eventually followed, causing Chester's population to swell each summer to roughly ten thousand. Former prime minister Pierre Trudeau vacationed annually in Chester. As did former MP Barbara McDougall. Sir Christopher Ondaatje, Sri-Lankan-born Canadian financier, philanthropist, and author, started coming in the early 1990s. He owned Meisners Island, situated just beyond Chester Harbour, for many years, and at one point, bought four other islands. He has also been a noted philanthropist for the village in numerous ways.

Part of the appeal of this village is the sheltered bay which has 365 islands, one for every day of the year, according to locals. There is a front and back harbour, providing lots of space for boats, docks, and boathouses. The waters are not over-crowded with sailboats as similar places in the United States would be, even though the expanse of sea offers ideal sailing conditions. Chester Race Week, which takes place in August every year, dates back to 1904 and is the largest keelboat regatta in North America. That's about the only time one sees a lot of boats on the water and activity in the village, which has often been the set for movies. Kirk Douglas, Sandra Bullock, Kathy Bates, Sean Penn—they have all starred in movies shot here. The village has a New England vibe and charming cedar-shingled houses, many surrounded by white picket fences or rock walls, and gardens alive with blue and white hydrangeas, rhododendrons, weigelas, azaleas, and roses.

Our hunt for a house or land to build on began in 1988. Then, luckily, a local real estate agent told us about what he described as the finest piece of property in the area: a 5.5-acre parcel of pristine and undeveloped land at the end of Chester Peninsula. It would offer a perfect canvas for us to create our East Coast sanctuary. There was one problem. The land wasn't technically for sale. In fact, a list of eager buyers had been turned away over the previous thirty years.

The property was owned by Helen Wood of New York. Her lawyers initially refused to let me speak with her, but I knew this land was perfect for us, so I was persistent. To improve my pitch, I suggested that it would be selfish to keep the whole parcel for myself, explaining that I wanted to subdivide the property and sell sections. I'd carve off two lots of 1 acre each and keep the remaining 3.5 acres at the point for my family, with a promise to not subdivide further, I told her. The result? She agreed to sell the land for $450,000.

I sold the two subdivided lots for a combined $450,000, meaning I essentially got the point for free! Securing the property, however, was straightforward compared to the challenges of building on it. To start, I had to fight nearby homeowners who opposed my plan to subdivide the lot and build extensively on it. The narrow, private lane leading to the property was not suited for the construction crew and trucks involved in building our house. But in the end, the plans went through, and we constructed our beautiful home at a cost of $1.5 million.

There were other problems we had to overcome. The house is perched above the water with a steep drop down to the shoreline below.

Erosion was a significant problem as the cliff face was receding by up to a full metre each year. I was determined to build as close to the cliff's edge as safely possible, so after clearing the land we installed a $300,000 Gabion retaining wall to stem the erosion, requiring nearly five hundred truckloads of shale and boulders.

In addition, there was no electricity running to the property. Initially, I agreed to bury the necessary power lines but then reneged when other residents, who would have benefitted from the upgrade, refused to contribute toward the $40,000 cost. After explaining my dilemma to a Nova Scotia Power vice-president, the utility agreed to run a new line to my property, which would skirt my neighbours by stretching for 152 metres along the shoreline—underwater. I personally paid the $12,000 to have the line put in with the understanding that any household at the top of the hill of the peninsula who hooked on would contribute to the cost. Which many did.

Then, there was the issue with fresh water. In Chester, there's no municipal water service. And there's little interest in having it, not only because of the cost but also because it would encourage development, something residents do not want. Most residents have wells on their properties. Those even sometimes go dry. It's not uncommon to hear of homeowners checking the level of their wells with a dipstick on a daily basis. Such are the quirks of life in a historic village! On the Chester Peninsula, the struggle to draw water from wells is greater than in the village. That's especially true for us at the point, which is rocky and elevated. Our solution was to install a seven-thousand-gallon cistern and filtering system.

As I often say, there's a solution to every problem. And I am always determined to find one.

Today, the property is assessed at $5.5 million but would sell for significantly more than that if put on the market. Built in a classic Cape Cod style as though the house had been there for decades, we continued the old-world ambience inside with lots of wood trim, high ceilings, dark wood doors, and hardwood floors. At twelve thousand square feet, the house has seven bedrooms, a living room, family room, expansive kitchen, an office, five fireplaces, two guest houses, a garden shed, an outdoor pool and hot tub, gazebo, a one-hundred-foot dock, and professionally landscaped grounds, featuring hundreds of rose bushes. Seven sets of French doors lead out to cantilevered decks around the house. Many of the thirty large windows look out at the sea.

Perhaps the best part of owning our property is being able to share it with others. We've hosted countless business partners, friends, and family members. For over twenty years, even though we are not sailors, we held a big party on the final day of Chester Race Week, watching the Princess Inlet Race from our decks with upwards of five hundred guests. There's no better place to view the fleet of sailboats (close to 150) moving around the different racecourses, particularly during downwind legs when the colourful spinnakers billow out in the wind. Our eclectic range of guests has spanned from politicians to well-known musicians such as Lennie Gallant, Jimmy Rankin, Terry Kelly, and John Gracie. At Christmastime, if we're in town, we host a large party for friends and family. We erect four huge Christmas trees in various rooms on the ground floor of the house. Fires burn in all the fireplaces. Outside, wreaths with red bows adorn posts at the gate and down the sides of the road to the front of the house.

If there was ever any doubt that this is our sanctuary where we can feel restored and protected from any problems in the world or in business, then wild storms rolling in from the Atlantic prove the wisdom of our decision. In February 1995, not long after the house had been completed, a mammoth winter storm pounded Nova Scotia. Bernardine was sure the roof was going to lift off. So strong was the wind against the house that our sons' beds were shaking. Everyone in the village feared for the safety of their homes. The wharf at the nearby Chester Yacht Club was destroyed. Shingles flew off many homes. Wharves were lost or damaged. A few small trees fell down around our property.

But we were safe. We knew we could weather whatever came our way.

The Jib, formerly known as Chesters, is a cozy coffee shop in the village where many locals and visitors come on a daily basis. People gather around tables to meet with new and old friends. Some people work remotely, hunched over their laptops. Sailors come and go, talking of their adventures on the sea. Kids scamper through to buy a drink or a snack. In a corner you might see a business meeting taking place as papers are passed back and forth. Gossip is exchanged. Problems are untangled in heartfelt conversations. Good news is celebrated. Even though there are other places to eat and drink in Chester, such as the popular Kiwi Cafe, I always feel that The Jib is the heart of the village with its casual, friendly, stay-as-long-as-you-like atmosphere. It's reminiscent of the fictitious café in Louise Penny's popular mysteries that are set in a small Quebec town, Three Pines. If there were a murder in Chester or some drama, The Jib would be where you'd go to find out the latest details.

At least twice a week, when I'm at home, I drop in for a coffee klatsch with some of the villagers who routinely meet to discuss world and local events. We talk about everything from President Trump, tariff threats, Prime Minister Mark Carney, his policies, whether we agree with him, the weather, house renovations, travel, and what we ate for dinner last night. Oh, and the weather. Everyone in the Maritimes discusses the weather as if it's a temperamental friend.

These groups, comprised of men and women from diverse backgrounds, provide me with a true sense of belonging. I love these impromptu gatherings, and my participation in them is partly why Bernardine loves to say that she changed my life by suggesting that we move to Chester. Laughingly, she says she saved me. She's right, I must admit.

Chester is a community in the real sense. Sure, there are online communities, and I'm not disparaging them. Human beings need to connect. But there's nothing quite like the comfort of a real-life, meaningful community. In Chester, people wave at you from across the street or cross it to say hello. At the post office, where all mail is delivered rather than to private homes, you often run into people you haven't seen in a while and end up talking about the deer who are treating your garden like a five-star buffet meal. If someone in the village has a problem or an illness, others will know and come to their aid. People find great solace and companionship through the many community events at the local playhouse, the churches (there's a Catholic, an Anglican, and a Baptist church), in one of the many community choirs, in a rug-hooking circle, an artists' group, at the Legion, one of the two pubs (the Fo'c'sle Village Pub and the Rope Loft), the yacht club, the golf club, or the Sunroom restaurant. For a small place, there's a lot going on.

Chester is an anachronism in many ways. It's as though time stands still. It is this yesteryear atmosphere and its slower, simple pace of life that draws people back again and again, a lovely and welcome antidote to the 24-7 hustle of the world.

And there are characters in Chester. I have become one of those characters. People know they can rib me. And I don't mind. Jim Barkhouse, a Chester resident and former provincial politician, sometimes says, "Please rise, everyone" when I come to join the morning coffee group. No one ever gets up, of course. Jim Cross, who has a company that has done most of my stonework over twenty years called last week and referred to me as "your honour." John Chandler, a Chester lawyer, often calls me Mr. Senator. It's endearing, always uttered in jest and affection. I love those guys.

I'm used to being ribbed. I'll never forget the time I was about to give a speech at an Atlantic family business conference with about five hundred attendees. Just before I was to take the podium, I walked round the room and stopped at the table of a friend of mine, Bob Belliveau, a litigation lawyer. I told him I was nervous about making my speech. Without hesitation, he turned to me and quipped, "Don't worry. People have such low expectations of what you'll say, I think you'll be just fine." I laughed. And I made sure to repeat what he said in my speech.

I don't take myself too seriously. I laugh at myself. Everyone in Chester knows everyone else's stories. They likely know that my one-time nemesis, Bruce Bowser, lives in Chester, a stone's throw from my house. We had run into each other many times since my departure from AMJ Campbell. We're civil toward each other, and I don't believe there's ill will on either side. In 2019, when I was honoured as the company founder at AMJ Campbell's annual convention in Montréal, Bruce sent me a nice note after the ceremony, which I greatly appreciated.

Many Chester residents know the story of building our house and feel no compunction about joking about it. Or, they read about the saga and the neighbours' complaints in *Frank* magazine. Many likely heard about my standoff with the local municipality over what I deemed to be excessive property tax increases. It was 1992, and I refused to pay my tax bill. It was too high. Our house had been assessed at $900,000. My tax bill was $9,139.35. Our taxes had doubled since finishing the house—a 100 percent increase in just four years! No water service. No public sewage system. The village didn't clear snow and ice in winter or pay for road lighting on the private gravel drive at the top of the peninsula. I was incensed.

I complained to the local councillor and threatened to sell our property over the issue. I had owned and lived in over nine houses at this point in my life, and I had never once felt the need to complain in this manner. I felt that someone should take a stand. The dispute was even reported in the Halifax *Chronicle Herald*, largely because everyone in Nova Scotia knows that Chester is filled with wealthy people. So, the idea that someone with means was complaining about paying taxes was a juicy news story.

I didn't care. My complaint was discussed at a subsequent council meeting. Eugene Brown, the councillor for my area, agreed with my statement. Clearly, an unspoken resolution was made. The next year, my assessment dropped from $900,000 to $760,000.

I am part of village lore: that guy who lives on the point of the peninsula in the palatial house at the edge of a cliff, who will complain about bills if he feels they're unfair.

Which brings me to a description of a large image that hangs on the far wall of The Jib above a table. A friend called me to tell me about it when I was in Barbados. It's a three-foot photo of a painting featuring a dapper-looking and well-groomed hare, dressed like a confident aristocrat in a tailored jacket with a jaunty pocket square and a gold pocket watch on a chain.

Under the picture is a caption that reads: "Tim Moore: 'A Self Portrait.'"

The owner of The Jib put it there.

And yes, I am one happy, unapologetic, thick-skinned hare.

Here in my sanctuary by the sea, and throughout the calm and turbulent periods in my life, Bernardine has been my anchor. I owe so much to her. How can I possibly express my gratitude to a woman I've shared a life with for forty-eight years? She has always supported me and looked after our family. She has followed me and stepped up to every challenge.

Several years ago, when we were meeting with our financial adviser, he was explaining about our investments and financial outlook.

Bernardine listened carefully and asked questions. We had always been very careful with household expenses. And then she turned to me, saying, "We've done better than I thought we had." She swivelled to look at the adviser and said jokingly: "Does this mean I can stop taking bottles back?"

I adore her. Bernardine is the most caring and selfless person I've ever known, not only my anchor but also my best friend. She always wanted a "normal and peaceful life"—something she never quite got—but she supported me in everything I did. I could never, not in a million years, have succeeded in life or business without her. She is the most important person in my life. We've been together for nearly fifty years now, so how is it possible that we are more in love today than we ever have been? She knows how to lift my mood with her silliness. Just the other day, when she got out of bed, in order to get me up, she started dancing around and teasing me. It was stupid and sweet; contagious and uplifting. She has done this many times.

We are a unit in everything. A few years back, as a major hurricane was pummelling Nova Scotia, Bernardine and I ventured out to witness the severity of the storm and see what damage might have occurred along the peninsula. Jumping in our truck and starting up the driveway, we saw a chair blocking our way. It had blown off the second level of our guest house. I put the truck in reverse and backed up. I then asked Bernardine to put the chair in the garage. She struggled to even push the truck door open and was nearly knocked over by the wind when she stepped outside of the cab. Her hair was flying all over the place.

Looking back at me, comfortable and snug in the truck, she smiled and said, "You're an asshole."

After moving the chair, she climbed back into the truck.

"In all these years of marriage, you have never called me an asshole," I said to her, somewhat chastised.

"Well, you are." A beat of silence followed. "A lovable asshole."

We howled with laughter as we drove up the driveway.

We have had our struggles. We have worked hard. We have made sacrifices. We have disagreed. We have argued. We have compromised.

We have lived, and we have loved.

Chapter 16
Guiding Principles

I don't think there's any skill more critical for success than resilience.

ADAM GRANT

Wharton School professor and co-author of *Option B*

THROUGHOUT THE YEARS, I'VE BEEN HONOURED TO BE named on numerous occasions as one of Atlantic Canada's top fifty CEOs by *Atlantic Business* magazine. It is meaningful to be recognized among my peers, especially since this part of Canada is home to many talented business leaders, many of whom I count as friends.

Each year's top CEO nomination has been followed by kind letters of congratulations. One in particular stands out. It was from Gerry Byrne, then an MP for Newfoundland and Labrador and Minister of State for the Atlantic Canada Opportunities Agency (ACOA), a federal funding agency. It sticks in my mind because of the importance that Byrne affixes to the top CEO honour.

"It is particularly significant, I believe, that this is not a list of people who head the region's largest companies, or those who make the most money," he wrote in his letter of August 2002. "Rather, the publication attempts to measure something less tangible but equally important. A key factor in their selection process is leadership, including industry and community involvement, as well as personal philosophy. The Top 50 CEOs are credited with displaying creativity, enthusiasm, innovation and steadfast dedication to improving the quality of life in Atlantic Canada. I commend you for your contributions to our region, through both your business and personal life."

As an entrepreneur who tries to add value to the community (while also making money!) such comments are very meaningful to me. It's always nice to have your contributions and efforts recognized. It's been especially rewarding to be nominated as a top CEO for more than one business (a rare feat.) I've since been moved to the magazine's CEO Hall of Fame, having secured a maximum of five top CEO awards.

I'd like this final chapter to close with a compilation of the principles and ideas that have most significantly influenced my career—the common threads that have tied all my businesses together. My hope is that you may return to this section as a quick reference and summary of the ideas I've presented throughout the book.

These are my guiding principles:

1. Know your business from the ground up and be hands-on.
2. Differentiate yourself from the competition. Look for ways to set yourself and your service or product apart from the rest.
3. Create a memorable look to make a strong impression.
4. Don't be hard on yourself for having false starts.
5. Always do what you promise you're going to do. You only have your honour, integrity, and credibility. Hold fast to this principle.

6. Exude confidence even when you don't feel it. Think of fear as a powerful motivator.
7. Be polite. Never raise your voice. Impeccable manners are key to success.
8. Never brag about your position, wealth, or possessions to employees, clients, or people in general. Humility is an enormously valuable trait.
9. Never consider yourself more important than another person. Always pay your way.
10. Think big, but act small. Always treat customers with respect and kindness.
11. Encourage key employees to buy shares. That way they're tied to the company and have a vested interest in staying for the long term.
12. Seek out mentors and positive people to surround yourself with.
13. Lead by example. Never ask an employee to do a job you wouldn't do.
14. Share honours and kudos.
15. Build relationships with your employees. Learn something about their personal lives.
16. Hire people based not only on skills but also on personality.
17. Walk the floors of your office daily to inspire and motivate your employees and to understand the soul of your company.
18. Create a corporate culture of inclusiveness, hard work, respect, and friendship. Always make time to thank your employees; it costs nothing and reaps rewards.

19. Address problems head-on and quickly.
20. Have a one-hour rule for dealing with customer complaints. Ensure that someone returns the customer's call within one hour to at least let them know you are working on resolving their problem.
21. Be a friend to the competition. Don't criticize them.
22. Never burn bridges.
23. Engage with your community through philanthropy.
24. Find three or four things daily that put a smile on your face and make you feel good. I'm a bit of a "gym rat;" I work out almost every day. I also enjoy my coffee group on a regular basis.
25. Live life. Have fun. Laugh. Enjoy the ride.

Acknowledgements

THIS BOOK IS A RECOLLECTION ABOUT MY ENTREPRENEURIAL life and business initiatives over almost sixty years. Many people agreed to be interviewed to recall the culture, successes, and misadventures of the AMJ Campbell years, including Carol Davis, Jackie Stewart, Joe Gagnon, my brother Terry, Kim Boydell, Leo Thibodeau, and Barry Stanton. Those were crazy, fun years with wonderful, driven, committed, and hard-working employees and partners. No one person could remember all the stories. I am grateful for the time they offered to help with the anecdotes and insights into our shared success.

I would also like to thank my sons Matthew and Chris who helped clarify the timelines and genesis of the various businesses we started together, including Premiere Mortgage Centre, Atlantic Signature Mortgage & Loan, Oceanstone Resort, and Moore Suites. With a constant desire to innovate and start ventures that spoke to our entrepreneurial instincts, we often had numerous initiatives on the go at once. My sons are an integral part of my family and business life, and I am grateful for their interest, enthusiasm, and clear memories!

With respect to all my businesses, there are too many outstanding individuals to recognize here, but I'd be remiss if I didn't highlight a few of these superstars: Kim Boydell, Clint Giffin, Jason Buchanan, Keith and Dave Dexter, Pierre Frappier, Lois Peterson, Jessica Brown, Sue Bachur, Jackie Stewart, Doug and Donna Auld, Hege Haslie, Neil West, and my family members. Of course, there are some very special people, my "unsung heroes" whom I would like to acknowledge. The first is my wonderful mother, June Moore, now departed but never forgotten. She instilled in me basic decency and compassion for others. My father, Tim, who was a good human being who instilled in us a strong family spirit and a deep-rooted value system. And Bernardine, who in addition to supporting me, has done double duty through the years as a mother and temporary father to our sons, Matthew and Christopher. She has done a wonderful job in raising them. The boys share their mother's intelligence, generosity of spirit, and kindness. That's all a man could ask of his children. I share her pride in them. And as if I'm not lucky enough, Bernardine's family and siblings are all exceptional, respected, kind, and professional people: Mark (Jay), Anita (Paul, deceased), Brian (Margie), Carey (Judy), and Bishop Daniel Bohan, deceased 2016.

For the chapter about the succession drama of AMJ Campbell and Bruce Bowser, I am appreciative of the professional legal advice from respected law firms. That period in my business life was filled with shock about the way events unfolded. I wanted to set the record straight about how I felt at the time and the unfortunate decisions and actions taken by Bruce that made my exit from my beloved company so emotionally difficult. The media can only ever get a fraction of the truth, and I am pleased that my lawyers helped me chronicle that period responsibly and accurately.

For his work researching and writing this book, I would like to thank Quentin Casey, a Nova Scotian business journalist and author of *Net Worth*, a biography of John Risley, co-founder of Clearwater Seafoods and a billionaire entrepreneur. Quentin diligently sourced material from newspaper and magazine articles, my two previous books, the court cases about Bruce Bowser, and from interviews. Sarah Hampson, bestselling author and award-winning former *Globe and Mail* columnist and feature writer, who is a new neighbour of mine in Chester, helped capture my personality and voice on the page. Also thanks are due to Kim Pittaway, award-winning journalist, author, and cohort director in the MFA in Creative Nonfiction program at the University of King's College in Halifax, who offered a manuscript assessment and suggested final touches to the book.

I am grateful to Nimbus Publishing for their editorial input and superb production. I thoroughly enjoyed dealing with them.

I must acknowledge some individuals and friends who have had a profound influence on my life in so many different ways. The Honourable Stephen Lewis, Allen Church, Sandra Smith, Barry Stanton, Bob and Susan Belliveau, Larry and Pat Pringle, Dave and Carol Hilchey, Murray Rich, the Honourable Myra Freeman and her husband, Larry Freeman, John and Susan Chandler, Jeanne Beker and her partner, Iain MacInnes, John Fitzpatrick, the Honourable Mike Savage, Richard Zuliani, Fred Smithers, and Kim Boydell, to mention a few. I am also grateful for my good-natured and ribbing coffee group, again far too many to mention, but which includes Jim Barkhouse, George Wilson, Derek Wells, Frank Metzger, Kathy Ross, Dave Dobrosky, Bill Hilchie, Brian Jackson, Mike Flynn, and Jean Nash.

One additional and meaningful blessing is that I live in the province of Nova Scotia where I have had the benefit and pleasure of interacting with some of the most professional, world-class talent in a cross section of business sectors. To name only a few: developer and contractor Joe

Ramia; builders Jim and John Kanellakos; developer Louie Lawen; realtors Sandra Bryant and David Dunn; Hakan Uluer (restaurateur of The Bicycle Thief); and media personality Steve Murphy.

Finally, as always, I am indebted to my wife, Bernardine, who read all the chapters and offered her positive assessment, never telling me what to keep in or take out. Nothing of the happiness in my family life or the success in my business career would have been possible without her.

SÁNDOR FIZLI

TIM MOORE is an entrepreneur and founder of several national organizations; he has developed some of Canada's most successful businesses, including AMJ Campbell Van Lines, Premiere Van Lines, Premiere Executive Suites, Atlantic Signature Mortgage & Loan, Premiere Mortgage Centre, Oceanstone Resort, and Moore Executive Suites. He was profiled by Alan Gould in *The New Entrepreneurs: 80 Canadian Success Stories* and is the author of *You Don't Need an MBA to Make Millions: Secrets of a Serial Entrepreneur* and the bestseller *On the Move: How to Succeed and Survive as an Entrepreneur.*